Allen Carr

The easy way to
MINDFULNESS

Allen Carr

The easy way to
MINDFULNESS

FREE YOUR MIND FROM
WORRY AND ANXIETY

To Sam Carroll, our candle in the wind

And to Emma Hudson, not only a fabulous member of our brilliant Easyway therapist team who have saved hundreds of thousands of smokers' lives, but also a truly inspirational sage of mindfulness

With editorial contributions from Tim Glynne-Jones

This edition published in 2017 by Arcturus Publishing Limited
26/27 Bickels Yard, 151–153 Bermondsey Street,
London SE1 3HA

AD005746NT

Printed in the UK

ALLEN CARR

Allen Carr was a chain-smoker for over 30 years. In 1983, after countless failed attempts to quit, he went from 60–100 cigarettes a day to zero without suffering withdrawal pangs, without using willpower, and without putting on weight. He realized that he had discovered what the world had been waiting for, the easy way to stop smoking, and embarked on a mission to help cure the world's smokers.

As a result of the phenomenal success of his method, he gained an international reputation as the world's leading expert on stopping smoking and his network of clinics now spans the globe. His first book, *Allen Carr's Easy Way to Stop Smoking*, has sold over 12 million copies, remains a global bestseller, and has been published in more than 40 different languages. Hundreds of thousands of smokers have successfully quit at Allen Carr's Easyway clinics where, with a success rate of over 90 per cent, he guarantees you'll find it easy to stop or your money back.

Allen Carr's Easyway method has been successfully applied to a host of issues including weight control, alcohol, debt, and other addictions. A list of Allen Carr clinics appears at the back of this book. Should you require any assistance or if you have any questions, please do not hesitate to contact your nearest clinic.

For more information about Allen Carr's Easyway, please visit **www.allencarr.com**

Allen Carr's Easyway

The key that will set you free

CONTENTS

INTRODUCTION

By John Dicey, Worldwide CEO & Senior Therapist, Allen Carr's Easyway

Life-changing moments don't come around very often, do they? In truth, we don't tend to go looking for them. While we bemoan the boredom and monotony of life and the repeat behaviour that leads us to despair, we tend to be sceptical towards any significant change – anything that requires us to alter our way of thinking. We assume that if wonderful life changes were out there, we would have found them by now. And so we end up leaving our happiness, peace of mind, and mental health to chance.

I was lucky. Back in 1997 I attended Allen Carr's clinic in London to see if he could help me quit my 80-a-day smoking addiction. I did so under duress. I had agreed to go, at the request of my wife, on the understanding that when I walked out of the clinic still a confirmed smoker she would leave it at least 12 months before hassling me about stopping again. No one was more surprised than me, or perhaps my wife, that Allen Carr's Easyway method set me free.

If I had been more open-minded, it would not have surprised me. By the time I went along, Allen had already helped millions of people to quit through his clinics and books. The evidence was plain to see but, being a nicotine addict, I couldn't see it. In hindsight, I can say that part of me didn't want to see it. It took my own personal, life-changing experience to convince me.

For a third of a century, Allen had chain-smoked 60 to

100 cigarettes a day. He'd tried countless conventional and unconventional methods to quit without success. Eventually he gave up even trying to quit, believing: "Once a smoker, always a smoker". Then he discovered something that motivated him to try again.

As he describes it, "I went overnight from 100 cigarettes a day to zero – without any bad temper or sense of loss, void or depression. On the contrary, I actually enjoyed the process. I knew I was already a non-smoker even before I had extinguished my final cigarette and I've never had the slightest urge to smoke since."

It didn't take Allen long to realize that he had discovered a method of quitting that would enable any smoker to quit:

- EASILY, IMMEDIATELY, AND PERMANENTLY

- WITHOUT USING WILLPOWER, AIDS, SUBSTITUTES, OR GIMMICKS

- WITHOUT SUFFERING DEPRESSION OR WITHDRAWAL SYMPTOMS

- WITHOUT GAINING WEIGHT

After using his smoking friends and relatives as guinea pigs, he gave up his lucrative profession as a qualified accountant and set up a clinic to help other smokers to quit. He called his method EASYWAY and so successful has it been that there are now Allen Carr's Easyway clinics in more than 150 cities in 50 countries worldwide. Bestselling books based on his method are now translated into over 40 languages, with more being added each year.

It quickly became clear to Allen that his method could be applied to any drug. The method has helped tens of millions of people to quit smoking, alcohol, other drugs and sugar, as well as to stop gambling, overeating, and overspending.

I was so inspired by Allen that I hassled and harangued him and Robin Hayley (now chairman of Allen Carr's Easyway) to let me get involved in their quest to cure the world of smoking. To my good fortune, I succeeded in convincing them. Being trained by Allen and Robin was one of the most rewarding experiences of my life. To be able to count Allen as not only my coach and mentor but also my friend was an amazing honour and privilege.

I went on to treat more than 30,000 smokers myself at Allen's original London clinic and became part of the team that has taken his method from Berlin to Bogota, New Zealand to New York, Sydney to Santiago.

Tasked by Allen with ensuring that his legacy achieves its full potential, we've taken Allen Carr's Easyway from videos to DVD, from clinics to apps, from computer games to audio books, to online programmes and beyond.

This book is an exciting, natural next step for us, in that it takes Allen's method beyond the realms of specific addictions out into the wider world – a world struggling to find a solution to the stress, anxiety, and pressure of modern life.

Allen always said his method was really about helping people to find happiness.

Addiction is a miserable experience. You feel trapped, helpless, foolish, a slave – caught up in an endless cycle of craving satisfaction but never quite achieving it, pulled this way and that between guilt, desire, and fear. Ring any bells?

Mindfulness has gained tremendous popularity as a method for coping with stress, anxiety, and depression. It is a broad term for an approach that can be applied and practised in numerous ways but, in essence, it is a method that echoes the principles of Easyway. Both work by unravelling the misconceptions that keep us trapped in a negative, harmful way of thinking. Both help us to see that there is more to us than our thoughts and beliefs, that our beliefs can be questioned, that body and mind are components of an incredible machine and, by developing a closer connection to our sensory system, we can maintain focus on the present and see things as they really are. Understanding is like bright sunshine that, rather than banishing negative thoughts and feelings, helps us to examine them, question their value, observe them, and let them go. When we are able to "not trust" our negative thoughts, to appreciate that we are not defined by them, it leads to a clearer, more positive mindset, reversing the vicious circle of negativity and setting in motion a new cycle of health and happiness.

Mankind has always been absorbed in the pursuit of happiness. The trouble is, the more we pursue it, the more it seems to elude our grasp. Why? Because we believe that control has to come through struggle. Our approach to stress is the same – and as a consequence life becomes a constant struggle. Allen discovered that it's the struggle that actually makes it hard, if not impossible, to quit smoking and other addictions.

His mindful method provided a different approach, one in which we let go of the struggle and, in doing so, find we are better able to take control.

For people new to mindfulness and Easyway, this principle can be hard to grasp. That's because we grow up brainwashed into a way of thinking that simply cannot comprehend how letting go can give us control; how willpower can be counterproductive; how we can push ourselves further with kindness and new understanding than with force.

Easyway has brilliantly transformed lives all over the world. The message to addicts is: you don't need a crutch; you don't need alcohol; you don't need cigarettes; you don't need refined sugar: you are fine as you are. You are perfect as you are.

At the heart of each of us is something that remains as pure and natural as the day we were born, but we live in a world that makes us fractious, anxious, agitated, and trapped. We have fixed ideas of how things are and are always looking around for something to make us feel better. But as our instincts are overridden by our intellect, it takes us further away from contentment rather than closer to it.

We all want to discover a better way of living, which makes us calm and contented. The key to happiness lies within; you don't need to cling to external "pleasures" – false pleasures that come with their own negative baggage. When you leave them behind, you're not giving anything up; you are only making gains.

Easyway has already set out a wonderfully practical pathway to help us free ourselves from our problems and addictions. It melts away the illusions that leave us prey to negative thoughts and desires. It shows us how we can gain clarity and control if we focus on who we truly are rather than being distracted by those things that harm and trouble us.

Mindfulness lies at the heart of Allen Carr's philosophy. The core principles of Easyway are those of mindfulness. Easyway has proved itself the world's number one method for overcoming addictions. It can also take us to a gateway – one that leads to a mindful existence.

I know from happy experience that the benefits of following this method can be life-changing. This book is the natural next step in Allen Carr's legacy, one that he mapped out himself.

It's my humble honour and responsibility to add a light editorial touch to Allen's work, to contemporize the anecdotes, examples, and subject matter for today's reader. Yet the method, the essence, remains the same – pure Easyway.

This book shares the proven principles of mindfulness and the proven principles of Easyway with a wider audience in simple, accessible terms that apply to real life and provide a tangible, practical outcome:

YOUR HAPPINESS

And now without further fuss, it's with pleasure that I pass you into the safest of hands. Over to Allen Carr.

CHAPTER 1
WHAT IS MINDFULNESS?

IN THIS CHAPTER
• THE ORIGINS OF MINDFULNESS • MODERN MINDFULNESS IN DIFFERENT FORMS
• MYTHS AND MYSTICISM • THE ROLE OF MEDITATION • MINDFULNESS IN A NUTSHELL
• ALL THE RAGE • EXERCISE: MINDFUL BERRY EATING
• MINDFULNESS AND EASYWAY

Imagine you could find a way to reduce the stress in your life, free yourself from anxiety, depression, and regret, and enjoy increased happiness and more peaceful relationships, while remaining calm and in control. Now imagine that, by achieving that happier mental state, you became less susceptible to sickness, injury, tiredness, and pain. If I told you that you have the power to achieve this happy state quickly, easily, and without making any sacrifices, how would you feel?

EXCITED? ELATED? SCEPTICAL?

What if I told you that millions of people have achieved their own state of happiness by following the method I am about to take you through?

If you're sceptical, doesn't it strike you as strange that you should regard happiness as such a difficult thing to achieve?

For such a sophisticated creation as humankind, wouldn't you expect happiness to be the default condition? As children, do we spend most of our time feeling unhappy?

Isn't it the case that life is more simple when we're very young, that we tend to live in the moment and leave the worries to our parents? It's only as we grow older and take on responsibilities that we start to feel the stresses of life and spend our nights wracked with anxieties that won't let us sleep. Of course, some youngsters are born into extraordinarily tragic and challenging environments, but it's only with age that these truly take their toll.

As adults, we tell ourselves we shouldn't worry so much, yet we feel helpless to stop. It's all easier said than done. In fact, telling ourselves not to worry often makes us worry more! We are so stuck in our way of thinking and responding to what life throws at us that we simply don't know how to change. We become blinded to the options available to us, especially the option of being happy.

That's right, happiness is an option. It's not a consequence of things that happen in life beyond your control. It's how you respond to the changing circumstances of life that determines whether you can be happy or not. And you *can* choose how you respond – all you need is a simple set of instructions to enable you to see that you have a choice.

THE ORIGINS OF MINDFULNESS

Mindfulness is a practice by which you enable yourself to see things more clearly, including the options that are available to you – in other words, to see things as they really are. The term has come to represent a meditative practice that dates back 2,500 years to the first days of Buddhism, and beyond that to the earliest yoga teachings thousands of years before.

The word "mindfulness" itself is an English interpretation of the word *sati* from the Pali language, in which early Buddhist texts were written. *Sati* is the first of the Seven Factors of Enlightenment in Buddhism.

Whether you consider Buddhism to be a religion, a philosophy, a way of life, or all of the above, it serves the purpose of offering a meaning to life and a template for living in a way that leads to enlightenment.

However, in Buddhism there is no god, and for this reason its teachings have captured the imagination of millions of people who seek a purpose but struggle with the concept of a supreme being. With Buddhism, the emphasis is not on pleasing God or some other deity but on sorting out the workings of your own mind.

Don't panic – I'm not going to suggest that you convert to Buddhism; it's just a way of explaining where the practice of mindfulness comes from and some of the history of the search for contentment. This is as old as mankind. Of course, all creatures – the lion, the tiger, the deer, the elephant, the gorilla – exist in a natural state of contentment without unnecessary stress and anxiety. That is, of course, aside from the thing that keeps them safe, fed, and alive: instinct.

Our modern understanding of mindfulness was pioneered by an American professor at the University of Massachusetts Medical School, called Jon Kabat-Zinn. He was a scientist who believed that by embracing some of the principles of yoga and

Buddhism and combining them with modern science, he could help people who were suffering from illnesses related to stress and anxiety.

In 1979, Kabat-Zinn launched his Mindfulness-Based Stress Reduction (MBSR) program and began to produce remarkable results. Today, the idea that stress, anxiety, pain, and even illness can be alleviated through mental reconditioning is generally accepted, and practices like yoga, tai-chi, hypnotherapy, cognitive behavioural therapy (CBT), and neuro-linguistic programming (NLP) are all common disciplines that take account of the power of the mind with regard to the wellbeing of the body.

Mindfulness takes that principle for treating maladies and applies it to everyday life, as a form of prevention as well as cure. The aim is to free yourself from the pointless, counter-productive, un-instinctive anxieties of life and enjoy a more relaxed, positive frame of mind, which in turn leads to better overall health.

MODERN MINDFULNESS IN DIFFERENT FORMS

Yoga and meditation lie at the heart of modern mindfulness, but they are not exclusively connected to Buddhist principles. Not at all. The ideas that the Buddha expounded were a development of something that we all experience from time to time, perhaps without realizing it, or stopping to fully appreciate it.

In the hurly-burly of modern life there are precious few occasions when we stop, do nothing, step away from the anxieties and regrets that race in and out of our minds, and tune in to the present. But those occasions do arise. It's normally in those moments that we come closest to our true "animal selves".

You've no doubt experienced the relaxing benefits of going for a walk. Walking has been shown to be a wonderfully therapeutic exercise. The mind begins to unwind, the thoughts and concerns that normally crowd in there are allowed to pass by, and we start to notice the world around us.

We become more creative as our minds switch from negativity to positivity. And we begin to develop a more realistic perspective. Walking has been shown to be conducive to creativity, problem solving, dialogue, and stress reduction.

Other forms of exercise can have the same liberating effect: swimming, cycling, and running, for example. As you focus on the rhythmic motion of the exercise and regularity of your breathing, the anxieties and regrets leave your mind and you enter a new, happier mental state in which none of those anxieties is a problem. You might think that you're merely being distracted from your worries; in fact, you're removing distractions and thus easing your worries.

As a child, did you ever lie on the grass and gaze up at the sky? How often do you do it now? Taking time to do nothing, to step off the treadmill, and allow your senses to focus on the myriad miracles taking place around you every second is another way to free your mind from stress and begin to see things as they really are. The cause of the stress doesn't necessarily disappear, but we stop ourselves getting hooked into it.

If you're religious, you will be aware of the mindful benefits of prayer. Prayer is a form of meditation. It involves taking time to find somewhere peaceful, close your eyes, focus, and let go. For people who believe in a god, the letting go occurs because of the belief that ultimate control lies beyond them, not with them. If you don't have religious beliefs, you can still experience the same sensation of peaceful letting go when you practise mindfulness.

MYTHS AND MYSTICISM

The point is, you don't have to be a Buddhist monk to practise mindfulness. If it is associated with mysticism and spirituality, that's simply because it is widely practised by people with religious beliefs. But they're not the only ones. Millions of people around the world have embraced mindfulness today in various forms.

For the majority of human history, religion has provided us with the regular opportunity to practise a form of mindfulness, whether in the form of prayer, quiet moments of reflection, or meditation. These days, the majority of people in the West no longer go to church on a regular basis, and so there is no time in our weekly calendar for stopping and letting go. We have become unfamiliar with such things, and so we're suspicious of them. We tend to regard them as hocus-pocus and become resistant to them, determined not to be taken in.

It's important that you don't regard mindfulness in this way. With practice, mindfulness is a tool for achieving a peaceful and ultimately a happy state of mind. For religious people, that means getting closer to God. For non-religious people, it means developing a better understanding of yourself and how everything in your life relates to everything else: a form of mental clarity that is available to all of us.

Doesn't that sound appealing? Remember how this chapter started: "Imagine you could find a way to reduce the stress in your life, free yourself from anxiety, depression, and regret, and enjoy increased happiness and more peaceful relationships, while remaining calm and in control." That is the purpose of mindfulness – it's not a religion, not a cult, not a quack remedy. It's a case of re-establishing the most natural, most instinctive mindset it's possible to have – one that was enjoyed effortlessly by early mankind and is instinctively enjoyed by the animal kingdom with which we share this beautiful planet. Indeed, as you will discover as you read through these pages, it is a return to nature's intended plan for you, a plan that has been lost amid the misinformation and brainwashing of modern life.

THE ROLE OF MEDITATION

Throughout this book, you will come across meditation exercises designed to help you practise mindfulness. Mindfulness does not rely on meditation, but it is a good way to develop your appreciation of the benefits.

With the forms of modern mindfulness mentioned earlier in this chapter, the mental benefits tend to happen as a happy consequence of the activity, rather than being the main focus. When you choose to go for a walk, swim, run, etc., you generally do it for the physical exercise first and foremost and the mental benefits are a bonus. With meditation, it's all about the mental benefit.

Ask most people to sit still, focus on their breathing, and empty their mind of other thoughts and they will struggle to keep it up for more than a few seconds. We are not used to controlling our minds in this way. Our everyday lives are full of distractions and our minds have become conditioned to leap from one thought to another, without ever settling for any decent length of time.

Therefore, we need a method to help us to calm this unnatural mental overstimulation and hyperactivity. Meditation is a method that can be practised anywhere, at any time, and without any need for special equipment, clothing, or gimmicks. Meditation is not praying. There is no god involved, and no cult rituals. It is something anybody can do and the more you practise it, the easier it becomes. You're not so much practising to acquire a new ability as practising to re-acquaint yourself with one that you, and your most distant ancestors on this planet, were born with.

It doesn't take up much of your time either. Just ten minutes a day is enough to make a difference. Just ten minutes in which you step out of the chaos, focus on something real, maybe your breathing, a sound, perhaps a sensation, and rediscover and develop the power of your mind, just as you might develop your muscles in a gym. In fact, it's not so much the power of your mind – it's the power of "now".

MINDFULNESS IN A NUTSHELL

So what exactly is mindfulness? What can you expect to feel when you become mindful? And how will your state of mind make a difference to what is happening to you in the real world?

There are many definitions of mindfulness. Here are a few that you might come across if you look the word up:

Awareness that arises through paying attention, on purpose, in the present moment, non-judgmentally.

Bringing one's complete attention to the present experience on a moment-to-moment basis.

The gentle effort to be continuously present with experience.

The practice of maintaining a non-judgmental state of heightened or complete awareness of one's thoughts, emotions, or experiences on a moment-to-moment basis.

Indeed, merely trying to understand the meaning of mindfulness from all these definitions can easily add to your stress, rather than dispel it!

Certain words stand out: "gentle", "non-judgmental", "present", "awareness", "on purpose". The significance of these words will become clear to you as you read through the book, but for now a simple definition of mindfulness will suffice.

The definition that I prefer is this:

SEEING THINGS AS THEY REALLY ARE

Perhaps you think that's too simplistic. Unless you're under the influence of mind-bending drugs, don't we all see things as they really are? We like to think we do, don't we? None of us likes to think we've been duped. But the fact is we can dupe ourselves – and frequently do.

Have you ever woken up in the middle of the night, fretting about some problem that's going to make your life hell the next day? You toss and turn, wrestling with the problem in a futile attempt to think of a solution. The more you wrestle, the more fretful you become.

You try to force it out of your mind, but it won't leave you alone. Eventually fatigue takes over and you finally fall back to sleep. When you wake up in the morning, the sun is streaming through the curtains and the birds are singing in the trees. You jump out of bed ready to face the world. And that problem that was haunting you in the night? Well, it barely seems like a problem at all.

The problem hasn't changed, you haven't done anything to alter it, yet it's gone from being a hideous demon that keeps you awake at night to being a mere trifle that you brush off in the morning.

At which point would you say you were seeing things as they really are? In the middle of the night when you were powerless to act and all you could do was wrestle with your mind? Or in the morning when you were free to do something about it?

This is one common example of how we fool ourselves into suffering with problems of our own making. Until we face our stresses by seeing things as they really are, we remain victims of our own anxiety. The more anxious we feel, the more stressed and depressed we become, which in turn makes us more anxious and more stressed and depressed. It's a vicious circle that can only be broken by stopping, reversing the process, and seeing things as they really are.

Mindfulness is not just thinking in the right way; it's the ability to be aware of your own thoughts. By observing your own thoughts non-judgmentally, with a feeling of kindness towards yourself, you begin to see them as they really are – mere thoughts. And you begin to see that your thoughts are not the definition of reality.

ALL THE RAGE

Mindfulness is enjoying a boom in popularity right now. It has come a long way from the 1970s, when it was often dismissed as the preserve of hippies, dropouts, and New Age oddballs. Since then it has proven its worth, to the extent that schools, prisons, corporations, and even the military use mindfulness meditation for everything from improving concentration and moderating behaviour to reducing the effects of post-traumatic stress disorder.

Increasingly, mindfulness is being seen as the antidote to a whole host of 21st-century problems: for example, the work-life balance, multi-tasking, peer pressure, cyber bullying, self-image, sleep deprivation, anger, tech addiction, and drug addiction. As we get caught up in the vicious circle of anxiety and stress, the need for a way to cut out the noise and find the mental space to think clearly becomes paramount.

According to numerous research sources, average stress levels are higher today than at any other time in history. We are afflicted by new illnesses and incidences of mental problems are on the rise. At the same time, we have become rightly sceptical about the reliance on pharmaceuticals to treat these conditions. There is a desire to find cures that don't involve drugs, coupled with an aversion to corporate control.

In short, there is a growing desire for peace, some respite from the clamour of modern life, escape from the vicious circle of anxiety, depression, and stress.

The good news is that escape is easy. By following a simple set of instructions, you can develop the ability to live a happy, healthy life.

EXERCISE: MINDFUL BERRY EATING

Here's a simple exercise to give you a first taste of mindfulness. This was used by Jon Kabat-Zinn early in his experiments with MBSR and it's designed to bring awareness to something everyday and ordinary – the eating of a berry. Actually Kabat-Zinn used a raisin but as anyone who has escaped sugar addiction using my *Good Sugar Bad Sugar* book will tell you, raisins are best avoided.

HOLDING

Begin by taking a single berry and holding it in the palm of your hand. Imagine you've never seen such a thing before, as if you're an alien who has just come down to Earth.

SEEING

Now look closely at the berry, exploring every visible aspect of it: the shape, the skin, the wrinkles where it's been picked from its stalk, the colour... Notice the way the light catches it, forming lighter ridges and darker folds. Take note of any unique features.

TOUCHING

Turn the berry over between your thumb and index finger, paying attention to its texture, temperature, and consistency. Close your eyes if you like and focus only on touch.

SMELLING

Hold the berry to your nose and steadily breathe in, noticing any aroma the berry might give off. Pay attention to any responses happening in your mouth or stomach.

PLACING

Bring the berry to your lips, noticing the movement of your arm and the precision of your fingers as you gently place the berry in your mouth. Hold it there without chewing and examine the sensation of holding it on your tongue.

TASTING

When you want to, start chewing the berry slowly and attentively, noticing how it needs to be positioned in your mouth for chewing and how your tongue and teeth work to achieve this. As you bite into it, pay attention to the texture and the burst of flavour in any juice it releases. Keep it in your mouth and notice any changes in the taste and texture over time.

SWALLOWING

When you're ready to swallow the berry, see if you can first detect the intention to swallow as it arises. As you swallow the berry, take note of the way your throat moves and pay attention to any sensations of taste or touch as the berry goes down.

By focusing on the eating of a single berry in this way, you are discovering the array of sensations that are triggered every time you eat but go largely unnoticed because of all the distractions. Think about the way you normally eat. Do you take the time to really taste your food?

Mindful eating reintroduces us to our senses and creates a surprising awareness of what we eat and our relationship to it. The result is a much more vivid perception of food. You might find that you don't actually like the taste of the berry… or, more likely, you might find that it tastes better than you ever realized.

Try this technique with other foods. See if it makes a difference to your perception of the foods.

The normal tendency is to bolt foods down fast, especially junk food, desserts, and chocolate, to the extent that we don't actually taste the food at all. We only think it tastes delicious because we've been conditioned to believe so.

MINDFULNESS AND EASYWAY

Allen Carr's Easyway is a method that has helped tens of millions of people around the world conquer addictions such as smoking, drinking, gambling, and junk eating by helping them to change the way they think and see things as they really are.

Easyway works by unravelling the brainwashing that leads to addiction and replacing it with a genuine perception of the truth.

When you start to see your addiction for what it really is, it becomes impossible to remain addicted.

Easyway also removes the belief that addiction is somehow a weakness in the addict. Rather, it is the consequence of a set of circumstances for which the addict was not responsible, and therefore there is no reason for blame and self-loathing. When you begin to see this, your whole mindset towards your addiction changes and the illusions that make it seem impossible to quit fall away.

Neither I nor any of my team of senior Easyway therapists who developed the method with me were mindfulness practitioners, yet the method, which is formed from an understanding of instinct over intellect and bound together by simple logic and clarity of thought, unknowingly applied some of the fundamental principles that are encapsulated in mindfulness.

As the lesson of mindful eating shows us, we do many everyday things in life without paying attention to them.

The same applies to addictions like smoking, drinking, gambling, and overeating. When we open our minds to the possibility that we don't do these things because we like them but simply because we have been fooled by a sinister combination of addiction and brainwashing, we can begin to develop an awareness of our own thoughts and actions, which leads to a change in perception – a start to seeing things as they really are.

As I will explain in the next chapter, the Easyway method has proven effective not just for people who want to quit smoking and other addictions, but also for tackling the worries of everyday life. The aim of this book is to integrate the principles of mindfulness with the Easyway method to help you make the changes you want in your life.

SUMMARY

- There is a method for reducing stress and anxiety, alleviating depression, and finding happiness quickly, easily, and without making any sacrifices

- You don't have to be religious to fully understand and adopt this method

- Meditation complements the development of mindfulness

- The aim of mindfulness is to see things as they really are – by paying attention

- Practise paying more attention to everyday actions

- Allen Carr's Easway is mindfulness in action

CHAPTER 2
AN INTRODUCTION TO EASYWAY

IN THIS CHAPTER
• Easyway's "Eureka" moment • A method that works
• Not just a cure for smoking • Alleviating stress and anxiety
• No need for willpower • The instructions

EASYWAY'S "EUREKA" MOMENT

Allen Carr's Easyway achieved fame as a unique method for quitting smoking. It was a method that went against the perceived wisdom of all other methods: it required no willpower, no substitutes, and no painful withdrawal period. In fact, I went as far as to claim that, with this method, quitting smoking was easy. It's a claim that's supported by tens of millions of people who discovered that what I say is true. There's a reason the method is called Easyway.

I was under no illusion as to how hard quitting smoking could be. I'd tried and failed many times myself. Despite the warnings of doctors about all the horrible things that would happen if I didn't stop, and despite already showing some of the symptoms that bore out those warnings, I found it impossible to quit permanently.

Eventually my willpower would always give out and I'd be dragged back into the nicotine trap every time.

I desperately wanted to stop. I was smoking 60–100 a day and suffering the daily misery and despair of being a slave to cigarettes. I had a permanent cough and suffered regular headaches and chest pains. I could see the agony I was causing my wife, Joyce, and it tormented me to think I was powerless to prevent it. In short, I knew very well that smoking was killing me but couldn't seem to find the strength to stop.

With my options running out, I took Joyce's desperate advice and went to see a hypnotist. The hypnosis did nothing for me, but a chance remark the hypnotist made, and a conversation later on with my son, caused me to exclaim to Joyce:

"I'M GOING TO CURE THE WORLD OF SMOKING!"

It was a classic "Eureka!" moment, as if a door had been opened in my mind, casting a ray of light on a beautiful truth that had existed all along but had been hidden from me by a curtain of darkness. This door represented the way out of a prison cell and I could now see it so clearly I could barely contain my excitement. And what was that simple truth that became clear to me? I was…

ADDICTED TO NICOTINE

Up until then I'd always assumed that smoking was a habit I couldn't shake because of something lacking in my physical or mental make-up. I had never thought of myself as an addict. The word was one normally applied to poor, washed-up people hooked on heroin, not those who "enjoyed" the "popular", "socially acceptable" cigarette. But hearing those words opened a prison door in my mind.

It was an easy step for me to see my predicament in the same way as I perceived that of a heroin addict. I wasn't smoking for pleasure or as a crutch as I had always believed; I was taking nicotine to relieve the empty, insecure feeling of withdrawal from the previous fix. It was the fact that the previous fix created the discomfort rather than the current fix relieving it which was a revelation.

Until then I had always feared that if I quit smoking I would be depriving myself of a pleasure or crutch. Whenever I tried to quit, I felt so miserable about missing out on that pleasure or crutch that I could only bear it for a limited time.

Now, all of a sudden, I could see that the pleasure was an illusion – just like the "pleasure" a junkie feels when he finally gets his fix. It was nothing more than partial relief from a pain brought about by the drug.

It occurred to me that was like the relief you feel when you take off a pair of tight shoes at the end of a long day. Continuing to smoke was as senseless as deliberately wearing tight shoes just to get the relief of taking them off. In an instant, it became obvious that there was no reason to smoke at all. It was also now clear that my previous failures to quit were not down to a personal flaw or weakness, but to the fact that I was caught in a trap – a particularly fiendish trap in which the victim mistakenly seeks release by turning to the very thing that is holding them prisoner.

The solution was glaringly obvious; all I had to do was stop taking the drug.

This was a revelation. I quit straight away without using any willpower, and I never felt the need or desire to smoke again.

To non-smokers, this solution appears so glaringly obvious that it's hard to understand why all smokers can't see it. But the nicotine trap thrives on brainwashing and all smokers are brainwashed into believing that smoking gives them some sort of pleasure or crutch. When you're in the nicotine trap, it's very hard to see the trap you're in. And worst of all,

NOBODY TELLS YOU

I made up my mind to change this. Thanks to a couple of chance remarks, I'd been able to see the situation as it really was. Now I was determined to share my good fortune with the rest of the world.

A METHOD THAT WORKS

After testing out my theories on some friends who smoked, I quit my job as an accountant and set up a clinic in my house in south-west London. Demand grew so quickly that before long I had to find larger premises and could no longer work from home. To this day, Easyway's worldwide headquarters, and main London clinic, stand a few minutes' walk from where it all started – in Raynes Park, London.

I soon realized that I wouldn't ever be able to help all the millions of unhappy smokers who wanted to quit by working with each one in person, so I published the method in a book, *The Easy Way to Stop Smoking*. The book became a bestseller around the world, and remains so to this very day.

The success of the method wasn't due to any clever advertising – I didn't really need to advertise. The success of the method was its own advert and endorsement. Long before the advent of social media, word spread across the globe that this was a method that really worked, a genuine solution from a man who genuinely understood the problem. When you attended an Easyway clinic or read *The Easy Way to Stop Smoking*, you knew that it was coming from someone who had lived through the nightmare of nicotine addiction, smoking 60 to 100 cigarettes a day, terrified of the effect it was having on his health but also terrified of life without his little crutch, and thus experiencing the same sense of failure and self-recrimination as every other smoker who tries to quit with willpower.

To this day, the people I've entrusted across the world to deliver the method in our live seminars are all former smokers who used the method to quit. Their main qualification is the years they spent failing to quit smoking and the fact that with Easyway they were finally set free. There simply isn't any way that someone who never smoked can properly relate to the experiences of the smokers who seek our help.

The approach appealed to smokers in a way that no other quit smoking method had done before. They didn't feel they were being browbeaten or henpecked; they weren't being told to grit their teeth and try harder; they weren't being made to feel foolish or weak; and they weren't being blinded with science either.

All I did was set out a simple set of instructions, which, if followed correctly, would open that prison door in the mind of each smoker who followed the method.

The Easy Way to Stop Smoking was the first of many bestselling Easyway books and Easyway centres are now established in more than 50 countries worldwide.

The method spread like wildfire for one simple reason:

IT WORKS!

NOT JUST A CURE FOR SMOKING

As *The Easy Way to Stop Smoking* sold around the world, I was convinced it could work beyond the scope of smoking. I noticed that a number of the people who were coming to Easyway clinics seeking help to quit smoking were also struggling with other addictions and issues: alcohol and other drugs, gambling, overeating, and even fear of flying.

The more I thought about it, the more it seemed obvious that Easyway was more than just a cure for smoking – it could be applied to any form of addiction. In fact, it went beyond that. In its essence, it was a recipe for a happy life.

Easyway has since proven effective in helping people to quit drinking, gambling, overspending, overeating, and even worrying.

All these conditions stem from the same source: a subtle combination of addiction and brainwashing. It's brainwashing that makes us believe that smoking, drinking, gambling, eating junk food, buying luxuries, etc., will make us happy. And it's brainwashing that makes us fear that life without them will be miserable.

Easyway works by laying down a set of instructions and it is crucial that you follow all the instructions in order. The trap of addiction works like a noose that gets tighter the more you struggle, but which loosens if you relax and remain calm. When you're in the trap, it's very hard to see the logic in this. That's where the instructions come in. They help you overcome your scepticism. It doesn't take long before you start to see how Easyway is working for you, but until you can you need to follow the instructions, regardless of any doubts. The only way to escape is to accept that what you believe to be the way out may not be the way out at all.

Once you have accepted this, you can begin to examine your preconceptions and dispel them one by one. This requires you to look at your beliefs with a questioning mind. For example, you've always believed that you smoke because you like the taste. By paying attention to your next cigarette, in just the same way as you paid attention to the berry in the mindful tasting exercise in the last chapter, you begin to see things as they really are. The cigarette does not taste good. In fact, it tastes foul. The first cigarette you ever smoked tasted foul too.

The only reason you changed to believe it tasted good is because you became addicted to nicotine and were subjected to massive brainwashing which led to you overcoming your body's natural revulsion by repeatedly smoking. You believed that was proof that you were "acquiring the taste". In fact, you were acquiring a lack of taste.

Most anti-addiction methods encourage the sufferer to resist temptation. With Easyway, you remove temptation altogether. As you unravel the brainwashing, so you remove the desire for whatever it is that you're addicted to. When you can see that it does nothing for you whatsoever, that the physical addiction is actually incredibly weak, and that by quitting you are not "giving up" anything, you have no reason left to want it.

But there is still a lingering reason you might not find it easy to quit. Even when you can see that your addiction gives you no pleasure or crutch, the thought of life without it can still be daunting. There are still some fragments of brainwashing that need to be removed, so you can see that life free from your addiction will be happier in every way. Again, Easyway encourages you to examine your preconceptions and test their logic. For some people, these final illusions melt away and they can't wait to quit. For others, they approach the moment to quit with some lingering doubts, but as soon as they stop they find the proof they need.

ALLEVIATING STRESS AND ANXIETY

As soon as you stop, the vicious circle of anxiety and stress stops. In its place comes a virtuous circle of clarity and relaxation. Any remaining thoughts that life without your addiction will be miserable are quickly dispelled. The last obstacle to freedom has been removed without any need for willpower and without relying on substitutes, which actually make it harder to quit, not easier. You don't have to wait for anything.

Unlike the willpower method, which leaves you wrestling with your desire to fall back into the trap, Easyway leaves you mentally prepared for life without addiction. That mental preparation is mindfulness: developing an awareness of your own thoughts, actions, and the world in which they occur in a way that enables you to see things as they really are and make sound decisions based on facts rather than illusions.

This is the very opposite of brainwashing. It's counter-brainwashing. It is pure-mindedness, a reversion to the way your mind was before it became polluted by brainwashing. All smokers are non-smokers before they start smoking; all heroin addicts are non-addicts before they get hooked on heroin; all gamblers are non-gamblers until they fall into the gambling trap; and all worriers are non-worriers until they get caught up in the cycle of anxiety and stress.

NO NEED FOR WILLPOWER

The outstanding selling point of Easyway was the fact that it did not require willpower. In this regard, it was different from all other quit smoking methods. Indeed, that is still the case.

Easyway's claim that you didn't need willpower at all in order to quit was not a gimmick, it was an essential part of the method.

The fact is that willpower isn't just unnecessary, it is actually a hindrance to any attempt to quit. The application of willpower is like King Canute's attempt to turn back the tide. It is a misguided effort to control a situation that has the natural tendency to run against your will. The more you struggle, the bigger the problem becomes.

Willpower is a finite resource and, regardless of who you are, it will eventually give out. When it does, you will find yourself more deeply trapped than ever before. There is a more detailed explanation of this later in this book.

What Easyway showed is that there is a gentler, easier way to free yourself from the misery of addiction – or indeed any other misery.

It involves a change of mindset, paying attention to the things that are troubling you in a non-judgmental way, not grasping and fighting to control them but merely observing them and seeing them for what they are.

This "letting go" is the essence of mindfulness. When you

open your mind to the possibility that what you perceive to be your escape route to freedom may not be the way out at all, you can begin to change your whole mindset towards whatever may be troubling you.

THE INSTRUCTIONS

To begin with, however, it's natural to harbour some scepticism. That's absolutely fine. In fact, it's essential. It will not prevent you from learning how to apply mindfulness and Easyway to achieve happiness. In order to help you past your scepticism, this book contains a set of instructions for you to follow.

FIRST INSTRUCTION:
FOLLOW ALL THE INSTRUCTIONS

That's all you have to do. If you reach the end of the book and you have followed all the instructions in order, you will be ready to enjoy the rest of your life, free from torment, from anxiety and stress, from depression, or any of the other man-made conditions that have become so prevalent in the modern world.

Perhaps you think I'm trying to control you. Perhaps the word "instructions" makes you think this is just another pressure in your life, demanding that you jump when you're told to jump. Rest assured, that's not the case. These instructions serve only to take the pressure off you. All you need to do is follow them and you'll be free.

Don't worry, everything *will* make perfect sense in time; you're not being asked to become a blind follower.

The beautiful truth that has made Easyway and mindfulness

such a success will become clear to you in good time.

With this method, there is no hardship you have to go through, no sacrifices to make. On the contrary, you have only marvellous gains to look forward to, so there is no need to feel anxious or daunted.

SECOND INSTRUCTION:
BEGIN WITH A FEELING OF ELATION

You have every reason to feel excited. You are beginning a journey in which you will discover the wonderful benefits of letting go. First, though, let's build a better understanding of exactly what it is you'll be letting go of. It's time to examine the brainwashing.

SUMMARY

- Until you see things as they really are, you can't change them

- All our anxieties stem from brainwashing

- Willpower is a hindrance to getting what you really want

- Scepticism is natural – the instructions will help you get beyond it

- FIRST INSTRUCTION: FOLLOW ALL THE INSTRUCTIONS

- SECOND INSTRUCTION: BEGIN WITH A FEELING OF ELATION

CHAPTER 3
WE'RE ALL BRAINWASHED

IN THIS CHAPTER
• MIND POLLUTION • WHO'S BRAINWASHING YOU? • THE VOID
• ASSUMPTIONS AND PRECONCEPTIONS • CONSTANT DISTRACTION
• INSTINCT VS INTELLECT • THOUGHTS ARE NOT FACTS

THIRD INSTRUCTION:
OPEN YOUR MIND

Perhaps you already regard yourself as open-minded. Over the next two chapters, I will demonstrate how most of the decisions we make in life are based on fixed assumptions, rather than an open-minded assessment of what we really see before us. As you read through the book, you will come across statements that you find challenging. Resist the impulse to reject them. Even if they seem far-fetched, open your mind to the possibility that they might be true. I assure you the truth will become plain as you read on and follow all the instructions.

Brainwashing is a strong word. It conjures up images of people being forced by evil scientists to wear metal skull caps and endure electric shocks to wipe their mind of vital information or input some kind of false information.

But the dictionary defines it as:

Any method of systematically changing attitudes or altering beliefs, especially one based on repetition or confusion.

This is exactly what we're talking about.

MIND POLLUTION

We are born without any preconceptions. Our minds are pure, receptive, and ready to absorb information at an incredible rate. In the first five years, our brains develop faster than at any other stage of life. By the age of seven, we have built up a vocabulary of between 5,000 and 7,000 words.

From the day we are born, we are bombarded with information and our capacity to take it in is incredible. We are taught how and when to speak, to listen, to walk, to eat. We go to school and learn about nature, science, languages, history, religion. We are taught what is right and what is wrong – a snowstorm of facts and figures for our developing brains to absorb.

At the same time, we are given life lessons: how to carry ourselves; how to treat other people; what is good for us; what is bad for us; what will make us happy, confident, popular, or successful… Amid all the genuine, valuable information comes a mass of misinformation that pollutes our minds.

By the time we reach our late teens, our brains have been polluted by countless thoughts, beliefs, ideas, statistics, anecdotes, and suppositions that are all presented to us as facts. Our view of reality is like a dirty windscreen, smeared with the dust and grime of the information highway, making it harder and harder for us to discern what is fact and what is fiction.

It is no secret that today the general public are deliberately being misled, lied to, distracted, and fed false information by people and corporations with vested interests. To protect their interests, the sugar and fast-food companies erroneously pointed the finger at "fat" as the problem behind weight gain and obesity. It's no secret that Big Tobacco suppressed the truth about the addictive nature of and harmful effects of smoking, or that Big Pharma have made a fortune by inventing (or as they'd claim "discovering") hundreds of "mental health conditions" for which they can sell a lifetime's medication.

You only have to look at the climate change debate to appreciate that there are people, corporations, entities, who are determined to convince us that black is white, that wrong is right   and that we can't believe anything we read. This mass of misinformation is designed to keep us trapped and destroy our spirit, so that we do as they wish. Now, more than ever, it's important to connect with our deepest, naturally inherited, and highly effective instincts.

It's no surprise that the most common addictions – smoking, drinking, overeating, and gambling – often develop in our teens, along with stress and depression. We can add to this the modern phenomenon of internet addiction. The brainwashing contributes to all these conditions and, once they've developed, makes them hard to kick. The only way to kick them is to unravel the brainwashing.

WHO'S BRAINWASHING YOU?

Some of the information we absorb as we're growing up is learned through our own experiences, but most of it is given to us by other people. First on the scene are our parents. From the moment we're born, our parents begin to feed us with information. They talk to us, which begins the process of learning vocabulary. They point things out to us and tell us what they are. They tell us when it's time to eat and to sleep.

As we grow a little older and develop the ability to express ourselves, they tell us when we're wrong. The information starts to be more controlling. Dress this way, talk this way, eat this way, sleep now, wake up tomorrow, eat this much, come here, go there... Parents have a huge responsibility to guide us through our early years, but the information they give us is not necessarily correct. In their efforts to control us, they will present us with "facts" to make us think the way they want us to.

"If you don't eat X, then Y will happen to you."

How many times have you been told something along those lines? Your parents will have been told the same thing by their parents and so on. And when you grow up and have children of your own, you hear yourself trotting out the same warnings. The message is so ingrained it becomes automatic – regardless of whether or not it's true.

As we grow older and our desires become increasingly at odds with our parents' desire for control, we start to question the information they give us – but that doesn't mean we begin to think for ourselves.

In place of our parents come friends, teachers, and idols, whose opinions become more important to us than those of our parents yet are no more reliable. We are still basing our reality on the word of others, rather than seeing it for ourselves. That windscreen is becoming increasingly obscured.

And through the fog comes another source of dubious information: the advertising industry.

Just as our parents have a desire to control us, so too do the sales and marketing executives whose job it is to make us buy products we don't need. How do they do this? By preying on our insecurities.

BE MORE ATTRACTIVE

BE MORE POPULAR

BE HEALTHIER

BE MORE RESPECTED

BE WEALTHIER

BE HAPPIER

The advertising industry is like one of those shady roofing firms that steals the tiles off your roof by night, then comes round offering to replace them for you by day. Advertising fills your head with false ideas about what is attractive, successful, happy, healthy, popular, respectable, etc., and then offers to sell you the solution.

And it uses your role models to complete the con trick. "You want to be cool and sexy like your favourite actor? Then use this perfume, this aftershave, this make-up, this fashion label, this shampoo. It's the one that they use."

I'm not suggesting you lose sleep over perfume or shampoo advertising. After all, if you've decided that you need shampoo to wash your hair then you're going to buy one brand, whether it's the one your favourite actor uses or not. With shampoo, the brainwashing is not harmful. But when it comes to smoking, drinking, eating sugar, gambling, and other activities that are proven to be addictive and highly damaging, we do need to be very much on our guard.

I have drawn a parallel between the influence of the advertising industry and that of our parents. There is one fundamental difference: our parents want us to be healthy and happy; the advertising industry just wants us to buy its products.

But just because the brainwashing comes from a different place, it doesn't make it any less harmful.

In fact, it's the more trustworthy sources that have the strongest influence. When a doctor tells you some "fact" related to your health, you're more inclined to believe it than if it comes from the man sitting next to you in a bar. The medical profession, governments, and health campaigners carry a lot of authority, which makes their opinions very persuasive. So when they get their facts wrong, the consequences can be disastrous.

A case in point is doctors telling smokers they need willpower and substitutes in order to quit. When the smoker fails to quit, does she tell the doctor he was wrong? No, she assumes the problem lies with her: either she lacks the willpower or she used the wrong substitutes, or both. Easyway enabled smokers to see beyond these assumptions, unravel the brainwashing, and walk free from the nicotine trap.

THE VOID

Insecurity is a natural human state. From the shock of coming into the world to the uncertainties of adolescence and adulthood, we are prone to an uneasy, empty feeling that drives us to look for reassurance. As babies, we look to our parents, but eventually we reach an age where we realize that not everything our parents have told us is true. The void begins to open up again and we seek other comforts to fill it.

We turn to our friends and role models for the reassurance we need. We need them to give us a sense of self, but it's a fragile dependency that often lets us down, leaving us looking for other things to fill the void. This is where drinking and smoking usually come in. Most often we are introduced to drinking and smoking by friends or role models, but they quickly become "our" thing. We smoke our favourite brand, drink our favourite drink. Unlike our relationship with friends and role models, we feel like we're in control with smoking and drinking. We decide when, where, and what we have and those drugs are always there for us when we need them.

As I will explain later in the book, the void is the empty, insecure feeling that keeps addicts coming back for more. The feeling you get from withdrawal is the opening up of the void; the "pleasure" you get from each fix is nothing more than a partial closing of the void. But each fix leads to withdrawal; therefore, every time you smoke, drink, gamble, etc., you ensure that you will suffer again.

The only way to fill the void with genuine happiness and security is to pay attention to reality and reconnect with the pure you that existed before your void was filled with brainwashing.

ASSUMPTIONS AND PRECONCEPTIONS

If, like most people, you eat three meals a day, it's probably safe to assume that those meals take place in the morning, in the middle of the day, and in the evening. The exact times differ from person to person, but they rarely differ from day to day. Do you ever stop to question why you eat when you do?

The likelihood is that it stems from your childhood. You will have been conditioned to eat breakfast, lunch, and dinner, and those meals will have taken place at practically the same times day after day after day.

You might ask what's wrong with eating three meals a day and the answer is nothing at all. There are plenty of people living happy, healthy lives on three meals a day. But that's not the point. The point is that we accept that way of eating without ever questioning it, which means we often go hungry between meals or, worse, we eat when we're not hungry.

Eating when you're not hungry is a sign of being disconnected from your senses. It is an example of the many things we do because we've been brainwashed into it, rather than listening to our senses and responding to our genuine needs.

Here are some other common assumptions:

SMOKING RELAXES YOU

DRINKING MAKES YOU HAPPY

SWEETS TASTE GOOD

YOU ARE WHAT YOU DO

Have you been taken in by any of these assumptions? Don't worry, you're not the only one. And you will soon be able to see the truth.

Brainwashed by the myth that smoking looks cool, stylish, or sophisticated, and offers comfort and relaxation, or indicates a strong identity, most youngsters try it sooner or later. Once they're hooked, a different piece of brainwashing kicks in: the belief that quitting is almost impossible.

This is enough to put off a lot of smokers from even trying to quit. The false assumption that smoking is hard to quit ensures that they remain forever trapped. Of course, the brainwashing is confirmed by their own experiences when they do try to quit. They find it impossible because they use the wrong methods. Eventually, they quit even trying to stop.

The assumption is reinforced by so-called experts, who state that quitting requires immense willpower. Because they're doctors and we have no medical qualifications, we bow to their superior knowledge and take their assertions as gospel. But there is a much higher authority to which we're turning a deaf ear:

OUR OWN PHYSICAL EXPERIENCE

When you stop and reconnect with your senses, it becomes easy to see through the brainwashing and begin to question your assumptions. When you take a mindful approach to your own actions you are able to see that:

SMOKING DOES NOT RELAX YOU – IT'S WITHDRAWAL THAT MAKES YOU TENSE

DRINKING DOES NOT MAKE YOU HAPPY –
IN FACT IT OFTEN MAKES YOU MISERABLE

SWEETS DO NOT TASTE GOOD – IT'S THE SUGAR
"FIX" THAT MAKES YOU THINK THEY DO

YOU ARE NOT WHAT YOU DO –
IT'S WHO YOU ARE THAT DEFINES YOU

CONSTANT DISTRACTION

Now that we all carry a communication device in our pockets, the bombardment of mind pollution is worse than ever. It was bad enough when our means of sharing information consisted of books, magazines, newspapers, TV, cinema, radio, billboards, and word of mouth. Now we have all those media on one device, together with the internet, email, text messages, social media, and gaming, all of which have the ability to intrude on one another, competing for our attention and ensuring that we never focus on one thing for very long.

This constant distraction is immensely stressful. It's rather like being in a box full of flies, all buzzing around your head, driving you to distraction. You can't focus on one thing or shut out the noise of the flies. There is a relentless pressure to keep up or miss out. Of course, in trying to make sure you don't miss out, you end up missing out on the most important thing in life:

HAPPINESS

When we're stressed we turn to distractions that require little or no mental effort – mindless TV shows, gaming, eating – and we stop questioning. We turn to these things in an attempt to escape from that box of flies, not realizing that they are actually guaranteed to keep us trapped.

What we need is something that will help us to see the box of flies not from the inside but from the outside. We need to lift ourselves out of the box in order to see it for what it really is – just a box of flies – and not a reality in which we have to spend our lives thrashing around.

INSTINCT VS INTELLECT

It seems paradoxical that human beings, the most intelligent species on Earth, should suffer and die from the consequences of stress, depression, and anxiety more than any other species on the planet. But the more you learn about the human condition and our susceptibility to addiction and depression, the more paradoxes you come across.

Why are we unable to use our intelligence to think our way past these problems? Because intelligence *is* our problem. Sure, it is the reason why we are the dominant species on Earth… but it's also our undoing.

Wild animals lead a stressful life. For them, every day is about survival. If they can't find food or water, they will die. If they eat something poisonous, they will die. If they are caught by a predator, they will die. If they don't protect their offspring, they will die.

Death is an everyday fact of life for the rest of the animals on Earth and yet it's man, for whom food and water are mostly in good supply and whose predators are generally kept at bay, that suffers the most with stress and anxiety, develops addictions and eating disorders, and, in some cases, loses the will to live.

Animals survive this daily dicing with death by trusting their instincts. They use their senses to find food and check that it's good to eat. They constantly look, listen, and sniff the air for predators. We have the same instinctive capacity for survival as other animals, but we also have the intellectual capacity to disregard our instincts. And somewhere in our evolution intellect has gained the upper hand.

Our intellect has given us the capacity to learn and pass on our learning. As a result, we've developed into a highly sophisticated species that is not only capable of building fantastic structures and machines, but also has an appreciation of art, music, romance, spirituality, and so on. Intellect is a wonderful thing, but it can go to your head. We consider ourselves above other animals and in many ways we are, but when it comes to eating properly and staying fit, we have a lot to learn.

The human body is an incredible machine with a remarkable resilience to the abuse to which we subject it. But there's a flaw in the machine, namely that we trust our intellect above our instincts.

We consider instinct to be animalistic, whereas intellect is sophisticated. But look again at the "advances" mankind has made and you'll see that, rather than building on the advantage that Mother Nature has given us, we've devoted a remarkable amount of intellect to self-destruction. By allowing our intellect to override our instincts, we've become a species of stressed, anxious, addicted, depressed, and violent junk consumers.

Without intellect, there would be no brainwashing. But we allow the brainwashing in because it seems more intelligent than following our instincts like an animal, and so we allow thoughts to intrude on experience.

A good example is the way smokers overcome the foul taste of that first cigarette. Anyone who has ever smoked will testify as to how horrible those first puffs are. Hardly surprising really – you're filling your mouth and nose with toxic smoke. Your body's natural defences scream out in protest: you feel nauseous, your eyes stream, you cough uncontrollably... and yet you come back for more.

If smokers listened to their instincts, they would never go near a cigarette again after that first traumatic taste. But such is the power of the brainwashing, feeding their intellect with false information like "smoking looks cool", they force back their body's protests and try again. Eventually, the body's natural defences stop protesting – they become desensitized, which means they are no longer functioning as they should.

The smoker now feels he has acquired a taste for smoking, but all he has really done is knock out his senses of taste and smell. The fact that the first cigarettes we smoke are so disgusting convinces us that we'll never get hooked. Most smokers who come to our live seminars can recall the warning from their parents about the dangers of smoking and their own reaction to their first cigarettes: "Ugh, I couldn't ever get addicted to this... it's disgusting."

It's only when we make our first attempt to quit, years later, that it dawns on us that we're trapped.

THOUGHTS ARE NOT FACTS

Putting intellect before instinct means we base our perception of reality on thoughts rather than experiences and as a result we become vulnerable to illusions. We create an imaginary version of the world based on brainwashing and take that to be reality.

We worry about things that are mere thoughts. Those fears that keep us awake at night are not reality. They may be triggered by real events or situations and real threats, but the fears we create are illusions; they are not real. Reality is what is happening to you in the present; the things you can see, hear, smell, taste, and touch. By allowing your mind to become obsessed with thoughts of regret (the past), or worry and anxiety (the future), rather than reality (the present), you invite stress to take the upper hand.

The level of stress that we suffer as a result of all the brainwashing we're subjected to these days is not what nature intended.

The good news is you don't have to put up with it. The belief that life is hard and we have to endure anxiety and stress is another piece of misinformation that keeps us from seeing our true potential for happiness.

Through mindfulness, you can reconnect with your body's natural mechanisms and start seeing, feeling, hearing, tasting, and smelling reality, while at the same time seeing your anxious thoughts as nothing more than what they really are: just thoughts.

I will illustrate where it all went wrong in more detail in the next chapter as I take a closer look at...

ADDICTION

SUMMARY

- **THIRD INSTRUCTION: OPEN YOUR MIND**

- We're exposed to brainwashing from birth, often from respected sources

- A lot of brainwashing preys on our insecurities. We *want* to believe

- False information becomes our reality when we don't question it

- The human flaw is placing intellect above instinct in importance

- You need to relearn how to listen to your instincts

- Remember, thoughts are not facts

CHAPTER 4
ADDICTION

IN THIS CHAPTER
• Symptoms of addiction • How brainwashing leads to addiction
• How addiction traps you • How illusions keep you trapped
• This sounds familiar • Seeing through an illusion

I first came up with Easyway as a cure for nicotine addiction. I then successfully applied it to other addictions, including drinking, gambling, overeating, sugar addiction, and overspending. With many, if not all of these problems, there has always been some debate as to whether they really are addictions.

Society tends to reserve the word addiction for drug addicts and alcoholics. In fact, there is no difference. Alcoholics are drug addicts. They are addicted to the drug of alcohol. Similarly, smokers are addicted to the drug of nicotine.

A lot of smokers dispute this. They believe the only addicts are the smokers who have been doing it for years and are smoking several packs of cigarettes a day. They don't see how someone who has only been smoking for a few months or years can be an addict.

It's only when you apply that reasoning to a heroin addict that they begin to open their eyes to the truth. We have no trouble accepting that someone who sticks a needle in their arm and injects a drug is an addict – why should it be different for someone who breathes poisonous smoke into their lungs?

Similarly, someone who gorges on junk food even though they desperately want to lose weight; or risks their entire livelihood on the spin of a wheel; or spends money they don't have on things they don't need – why should they be regarded so differently from the heroin addict?

Symptoms of addiction

All these conditions have the same symptoms in common:

REPEATEDLY DOING SOMETHING THAT MAKES YOU UNHAPPY

WANTING TO STOP BUT BEING UNABLE TO

REPEATEDLY TRYING AND FAILING TO STOP

DENIAL – LYING TO YOURSELF

DECEIT – LYING TO OTHERS

MISERY – FEELING LIKE A HELPLESS SLAVE

These symptoms will be familiar to a very large number of readers. If they apply to you then there is good news:

EASYWAY CAN HELP

These are the symptoms of addiction and they can apply to an increasing array of aspects of modern life. Drugs (including nicotine and alcohol) and gambling may be the two most recognized addictions, but these symptoms increasingly apply to food, sugar, money, work, relationships, the internet, pornography, etc.

All these symptoms are the consequence of intellect overruling instinct. What other explanation can there be for continuing to do something that you wish you didn't do and that makes you miserable? Nobody forces smokers to smoke. They choose to buy the cigarette, put it to their lips, light it, and inhale.

Drowning out the voice in their head that's telling them to stop is another voice telling them that smoking gives them some sort of pleasure or crutch. This voice is the result of all the brainwashing. Even when the signs of damage from smoking are so obvious as to be undeniable, the smoker will argue that there must be something about the cigarette that he just couldn't live without – otherwise, why else wouldn't he just stop?

The lack of logic is clear to anybody who isn't trapped by addiction, but when you are in that trap you stop seeing things as they really are and instead see things through the back-to-front lens of addiction. You find yourself caught in a tug-of-war between the fear of the harm you're doing to yourself ("it's costing me a fortune, controlling my life, making me and my family miserable and fearful, and destroying me") and the fear of having to live without your little crutch ("how can I cope, how hard is it going to be, how awful will I feel, will life be worth living, how will I enjoy life?").

Can you see that fear is at both ends of that tug-of-war? And can you see what causes the fear at both ends of that tug-of-war? It's the drug. It's this tug-of-war of fear that keeps addicts in limbo, imprisoned in the trap, and the only way to escape is to remove one half of the tug-of-war. To do that you need to unravel the brainwashing.

HOW BRAINWASHING LEADS TO ADDICTION

The brainwashing from advertising creates the false assumption that certain things give us some sort of pleasure or crutch. Pay attention to the content of advertisements. When a product has something of genuine value to offer, the advertising will focus on that particular selling point.

For example, apples are juicy, fresh, and packed with vitamin C. There is no need to spin a yarn in order to sell an apple – the benefits are obvious. Whisky, on the other hand, contains nothing of nutritional value. It dulls your senses and sabotages your mental and physical capabilities. That makes whisky a hard sell. So what do the advertisers do? They create the illusion of an appealing lifestyle. When people buy whisky, they're not buying into liver damage and inebriation; they're buying into Scottish moorland and cosy evenings by the fire. They've been brainwashed into believing that whisky completes the picture and, by inference, without whisky they are incomplete. But not just any old whisky – THIS particular whisky.

An old friend of mine who worked in advertising used to tell me: "You don't sell the sausage…you sell the sizzle!" and if you know what goes inside most sausages you'll understand why.

It's a clever con trick, which we fall for time and time again.

The myth of pleasure or a crutch is, ironically, reinforced

by so-called experts who tell us these things are not only hard to "give up" but attempt to explain why they're enjoyable. Endless studies about dopamine, serotonin, addictive genes, and addictive personalities simply serve to intellectualize why something addictive feels pleasurable… they don't set anyone free and simply reinforce the feeling of impending doom the addict feels when considering an attempt to escape.

It's simple. Addiction has got nothing to do with pleasure, and dopamine and serotonin don't matter a jot – in the same way as it doesn't matter what causes a sense of relief when you stop banging your head against a brick wall. The important thing is that you understand that by stopping banging your head, the pain disappears and never, ever comes back.

The term "give up" itself implies a sacrifice. And the more we're told that something is hard to quit, the more we assume that there must be something about it that overrides all the negatives.

Then there is the brainwashing from figures of authority: parents, teachers, governments. Well-meaning as these figures may be, their warnings create a taboo, which makes the subject more attractive in our eyes.

By the time we are old enough to start choosing the things we buy and consume, our brains have been bombarded with a combination of temptations and warnings about a whole host of things that do us no good whatsoever. Caught up in this fog of mixed messages, our natural curiosity drives us to find out for ourselves.

We are looking for something to fill the void and find ourselves pulled in all directions. We want to rebel against authority, conform with our peers, emulate our role models. We want to escape, fit in, stand out, disappear. We want to find our own identity.

From this fragile, stressful state, it's but a short step to addiction of one kind or another. Anything that promises to make us look cool while at the same time emphasizing our independence from our parents and other authority figures becomes very attractive. All too easily we wander into the trap.

HOW ADDICTION TRAPS YOU

Easyway explains addiction as the combined effect of two monsters: the Little Monster in your body (the withdrawal) and the Big Monster in your head (the brainwashing). Taking smoking as an example, the Little Monster is the empty, insecure feeling you get when the nicotine leaves your system. It's a very mild physical sensation, but it's enough to nudge awake the Big Monster. The Big Monster is the brainwashing. It's the voice in your head that interprets the cries of the Little Monster as "I need a cigarette".

One cigarette is all it takes to bring these monsters to life. The nicotine enters your system and the Little Monster is born as it begins to withdraw. The Little Monster starts to cry out for more nicotine and a new void opens up, making you feel empty and insecure.

The Little Monster awakes the Big Monster in your brain – the belief that smoking gives you some sort of pleasure or crutch and that smoking does something for you.

If you listen to the Big Monster and smoke another cigarette, you begin a cycle of withdrawal and fixing that takes you further and further into the nicotine trap.

That next fix partially relieves the discomfort of withdrawal, reinforcing your belief that smoking relaxes you and so strengthening the Big Monster. It seems to confirm the brainwashing: smoking seems to fill a void. But it was a void that nicotine created. Soon you're smoking whenever you feel unrelaxed. And because nicotine actually makes you more edgy, you feel stressed most of the time. Your descent into the nicotine trap accelerates.

It's like a fly on a pitcher plant, one of those carnivorous, funnel-shaped plants that lures flies in with their nectar and then consumes them when they slip into the digestive fluids at the bottom of the funnel. When the fly first lands on the plant, it has no idea that it's in a trap. It could fly away any time it likes, but the nectar tastes good, so it carries on feeding.

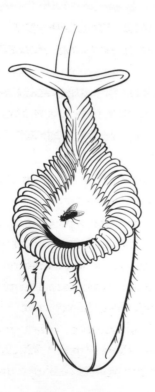

As it feeds, it wanders further in. The sides of the plant become steeper and more slippery. Still the fly keeps feeding until it feels itself beginning to lose its grip. Soon it's too late to fly away. The pitcher plant claims another victim.

Left: the pitcher plant

Like the fly, smokers aren't aware that they're walking into a trap when they first smoke. By the time they start to realize that all is not well, addiction has them in its grip. The more they try to escape, the tighter the bonds grow around them.

We are using smoking as our example; the same principles apply to any behaviour where we override our instincts and follow a path of self-harm.

THE BRAINWASHING SUCKS US INTO THE BEHAVIOUR IN THE BELIEF THAT IT WILL MAKE US FEEL COOL, OR STYLISH, OR GROWN-UP, OR COMPLETE

THE ADDICTION CREATES A VOID THAT WASN'T THERE BEFORE AND MAKES US SEEK SOME RELIEF

THE BRAINWASHING COMPELS US TO SEEK RELIEF IN THE VERY THING THAT'S CAUSING THE VOID TO EXIST IN THE FIRST PLACE; IT'S TRUE MISERY

So why does the addict not remain on the lip of the pitcher plant? Why does the situation always get worse?

Each fix brings relief from the Little Monster's pangs – but it is only partial relief. It doesn't completely close the void. If we consider our level of wellbeing without addiction as par on a graph, the first withdrawal takes us down below par. The next fix picks us up again but not far enough to get back to par.

The next withdrawal takes us down further than before and the next fix leaves us even further short of par. With each fix, we fall further and further below par. We crave bigger and bigger doses, which in turn create deeper and deeper lows. The physical effects add to the misery, causing a double low. And as we become increasingly aware of our predicament, the misery of knowing we're in a trap creates a triple low.

With the Big Monster ruling our head, the desire for our little crutch increases.

This is how addiction takes hold and tightens its grip. The natural tendency with addiction is always to increase the dose. It's only through force of circumstance (e.g. not being allowed to smoke at work or not being able to afford to smoke more) or strong self-control that any smoker maintains a steady level of consumption. That's why addiction makes its victims miserable: they are always having to deprive themselves.

ALL ADDICTS WANT TO QUIT

The trap is controlled entirely by the Big Monster that keeps you fooled into believing your addiction gives you some sort of pleasure or crutch.

It doesn't have to be a drug; it can just as well be an activity like gambling or chatting online. If you find yourself increasingly drawn to do it and you feel restless when you're without it, the addiction has taken hold. As long as you have the Big Monster in your mind, you remain a slave. The only way to escape is to unravel the brainwashing and kill the Big Monster.

HOW ILLUSIONS KEEP YOU TRAPPED

The brainwashing fills our heads with a lot of misinformation, but there are two powerful illusions that keep addicts in the trap.

THE ILLUSION OF PLEASURE OR A CRUTCH

THE ILLUSION THAT IT'S HARD TO QUIT

There are many factors that create and reinforce these illusions. The illusion of pleasure or a crutch is created by the storm of false information from advertising and the media, reinforced by the warnings from authority and the false testimony of other addicts. Unfortunately addicts always lie. They have to in order to justify why they continue to do something they know makes no sense. Rather than admitting that they're a helpless addict, they pretend to be having a great time thanks to their little crutch.

THIS SOUNDS FAMILIAR

As you become addicted, the illusion of pleasure or a crutch is further strengthened by the restless feeling you experience when you can't get your fix and the partial relief when you do. As long as you remain susceptible to this illusion, the Big Monster continues to control you. You continue to be deluded into seeking relief from the very thing that's making you miserable.

If you do make up your mind to quit, your decision is immediately tested by the illusion that quitting is hard. For many addicts, this belief is enough to put them off even trying to quit. They are caught in the tug-of-war of fear and the fear of life without their little crutch is stronger than their fear of the harm it's causing them. They would rather take their chances in the trap, even though they're consigning themselves to a life of misery.

Helping an addict to see through these illusions is key to their escape. When you're in the trap, you don't see the reality of your predicament because your mind is distracted by false assumptions. To anyone looking at you from the outside, it's obvious what you need to do to get free – just as it's easy for anyone observing a heroin addict to see that the only way for them to kick their addiction is to stop taking the drug.

But when you're in the trap, you tend to see things back to front. It's only when you take a mindful approach that you start to see the situation as it really is.

The second instruction was to keep an open mind. The illusions keep us trapped because we close our minds to the possibility that they might be false and that we might have been misled into a trap. Nobody likes to admit that they've been fooled. So rather than question everything we hold to be true, we close our minds and stumble on controlled by monsters and denying ourselves the chance of happiness.

When you practise mindfulness, you begin to gain clarity as to what is real and what is an illusion. This exercise will give you an idea of how it works.

SEEING THROUGH AN ILLUSION

Illusions can be fun, as long as they're not responsible for keeping you in a trap. Take a look at the two tables on the opposite page. Make a note of which is the longer, A or B?

Now take a ruler and measure the two tables. Surprising, isn't it?

What you're looking at is a famous optical illusion, whereby the tables are drawn in such a way as to look very different

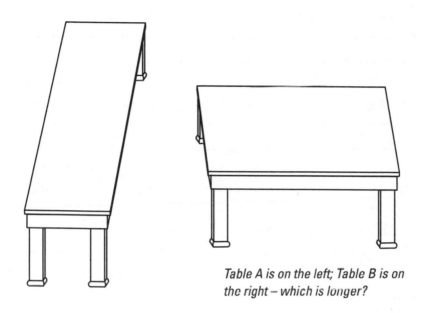

Table A is on the left; Table B is on the right – which is longer?

in dimension when, in fact, they are identical. Had you not been told to measure them you would have carried on with the assumption that they are different sizes.

Now try this. Look at the tables again and try to convince yourself that they really are different sizes.

Impossible, isn't it?

Once you see through an illusion and start seeing things as they really are, you can't be fooled by that illusion again. By opening your mind and looking at the situation from a new perspective, you obtain a realistic perspective.

This is key to curing the addictions that prevent us from achieving genuine happiness. Addiction is a big word but, as Easyway has proved for over 30 years, it can be overcome by changing your mindset and unravelling the brainwashing.

SUMMARY

- Addiction is a consequence of intellect overruling instinct

- In order to escape you have to kill the Big Monster that's created by brainwashing

- Addiction is a downward spiral because relief is never complete

- Each fix creates a greater need for the next

- Addicts seek relief from the very thing that's causing them misery

- A mindful approach enables you to see through the illusions

CHAPTER 5
UNHAPPINESS

IN THIS CHAPTER
• A GLASS HALF EMPTY • WHAT'S GETTING YOU DOWN?
• THE BOX OF FLIES • POUNCING AND HIDING • EXERCISE: THE BODY SCAN

We carry a lot of illusions around with us – assumptions and preconceptions that get fixed in our minds. Sadly, these assumptions and preconceptions have a tendency to be negative.

A GLASS HALF EMPTY

We've talked already about how intelligence is the flaw in the incredible human machine. It makes us susceptible to false information and overrides instinct to leave us vulnerable to harm. Intelligence also sets us apart from other animals in the way we are geared for survival. While animals rely on their senses to trigger the responses of fight or flight, we have the additional capacity to learn from the past and think ahead.

This intellectual capacity has made us very adept at averting danger, building defences, and militating against setbacks. But it has also left us with a tendency to focus on negative thoughts. Research has shown that when our minds are left to wander we actually become less happy.

Our intellectual approach to survival has conditioned our wandering minds to settle on problems rather than pleasures, for the simple reason that problems are more likely to kill us. We also learn faster from negative experiences than from positive ones.

Perhaps you're thinking the message I'm trying to put across is that we're all doomed to unhappiness because it's the only way we survive. Not at all. I'm talking about a mental conditioning that evolved in a time when life was considerably more dangerous than it is today, with the constant threat of attack from predators or death by hunger, cold, and natural disasters.

Times have changed but much of the conditioning remains. Scientists call it "the negativity bias" – the tendency to focus on our problems. The problem is that our minds don't just tend to focus on problems, they exaggerate them. We create artificial scenarios in our minds that cause us undue stress.

No doubt you've experienced the fear of lying in bed at night and hearing a floorboard creak. Your mind flies to the thought that there's an intruder in the house. Your heart starts pounding; your ears prick up; you lie dead still listening for confirmation of your impending doom. Despite the fact that very few people ever have an intruder in their house, it is in our nature to leap to the conclusion that every creaking floorboard at night is a threat.

It's a pessimistic approach to life that ensures we suffer regardless of how things turn out.

WHAT'S GETTING YOU DOWN?

We have much to be happy about these days. We live longer, find food and warmth easily, travel faster and further, and get to see and experience more. And yet all these things bring their own problems, which we tend to focus on: the incapacity of old age, the cost of food and fuel bills, delays on the roads, railways and airports, the fear of missing out on something.

Whatever life offers us, we seem to be able to turn it into a negative. And there are plenty of things in life that seem to present us with constant worries.

MONEY

Who hasn't ever had money worries? As the saying goes, "No matter how much you've got, it's never enough." The cost of living and making ends meet is a major worry for people from all walks of life. Even when we're able to afford a comfortable lifestyle, we worry whether we're living as well as the people next door or whether it will last. The money we earn affects whether we feel valued and how we value ourselves. We worry about making enough money to support our dependents. We even worry about leaving enough money for our loved ones when we die. We worry about having enough money to join in and to be perceived as generous. And if we should ever be fortunate enough to have more money than we need, we worry about sharing it with others.

WORK

We commit a sizeable amount of our lives to work and that's a sizeable amount of time spent worrying. There's the pressure to stay employed, which means dealing with the pressure to perform and meet targets. We worry about earning enough money, getting on with people, building constructive relationships, and climbing the career ladder. We feel the pressure of managing our hours, remembering all our obligations, and being on time. Which brings us on to the next ever-present worry.

TIME

Who invented time? Whoever it was, they didn't make quite enough of it, did they? How often do you find yourself wishing you had one more hour in the day or one more day in the week? Like money, no matter how much time we have, it's never quite enough. We all possess the same amount of time every day, out of which we need to find some for work, some for home life, some for free time and recreation, some for family and friends. We spend our lives trying to strike a healthy work-life balance, but there never seems to be enough time for everything we want to do.

RELATIONSHIPS

All of the above can have a negative effect on relationships. When you're stressed, it affects your relationships at work, home, and elsewhere. It also affects your relationship with yourself. You know when you're behaving unreasonably, but when you're feeling pressured by money, work, or time, it can be hard to change your behaviour. The way we interact with others and the way we regard ourselves have a major effect on our happiness. The slightest sign of friction can create the belief in your mind that someone dislikes you. When you feel a relationship turning sour, it creates additional stress, causing a downward spiral. This can damage your relationship with yourself just as much as one with someone else.

HEALTH

Medical science has made enormous strides in the last hundred years yet health remains a major source of stress. As laymen, we know a lot more about the threats to our health than our forefathers did, so we have more to worry about. We don't just worry about diseases, we worry about what we eat and drink, how much we weigh, what we look like, how much sleep we get… the list is endless. We can literally worry ourselves sick.

VICES

Then there are the things we do that we wish we didn't: addictions, for example, which we believe we're reliant on as an escape from stress. The fact that we can't get control of our vices becomes a cause of even more stress, which in turn makes us feel more trapped.

EVERYTHING ELSE

Even when we're feeling liberated from the common stresses mentioned above, other things can come along and push us back into a negative mindset. Politics, terrorism, a distant war, the weather…

THE BOX OF FLIES

There are enough pressures in life to justify the negativity bias. And yet research has shown that, in the first world, positive experiences outnumber negative ones by three to one. If our mood responded directly to the things we experience in life, we should spend three-quarters of our lives feeling happy.

But our minds naturally wander towards negativity and we become caught up in a downward spiral. When we feel low, we are more susceptible to worrying. The more we worry, the lower we feel. The worry itself becomes another source of stress, exacerbating the problem and making it hard to escape the vicious circle.

All the pressures and stresses buzz around your head like flies in a box. Instead of calm and relaxation, you are subjected to the constant noise of thoughts flying around your brain. You typically respond in one of three ways:

LASHING OUT

PRETENDING THEY DON'T EXIST

THINKING THEM THROUGH

Imagine swatting out at a swarm of flies buzzing around you in a box. The effect is futile. It only makes you more stressed. That's what happens when you respond with aggression to the negative thoughts in your head.

Now imagine trying to pretend there are no flies. You close your eyes and mouth, but you can't close your ears or stop feeling. This is what happens when you try to ignore the negatives. You're effectively burying your head in the sand. Again, it's futile. The flies continue to buzz around you and you can't pretend they're not there.

So you try to think up a solution to all the flies, but there are so many of them and they move so randomly that you're incapable of tackling them with rational thought. Despair begins to set in.

The good news is there is a fourth way:

MINDFULNESS

With the first three methods, you are trying to find a solution to the flies; with mindfulness, you are not. You are merely observing them without judgment. You are controlling negative thoughts – by letting them go. And as you let go, you find your mindset changes so you are no longer in the box surrounded by the flies but you are looking at the box from outside and seeing it for what it is: a box of flies.

Not a world of threats.

By letting go, you actually gain control. This may sound counter-intuitive, but that's because we are conditioned to think we can only control our problems by grappling with them. We assume that there is some external solution that we need to find. With mindfulness you learn that strength is gained through gentleness and the solution lies within your own consciousness.

POUNCING AND HIDING

The stressed mind tries to attain happiness by clutching on to pleasant experiences and avoiding painful ones. This becomes a constant struggle of pouncing and hiding, which is itself highly stressful.

Unhappiness becomes your default mode because you get stuck in a negative mindset. You don't pay attention to the reality of your experiences and instead struggle on, clinging to outmoded beliefs. It's like a pilot flying on an autopilot system that has been programmed for a completely different flight path.

If you looked out of the window, you would see the mountains looming up ahead, but instead you carry on blindly assuming that your automatic way of doing things will see you through.

We have developed this automatic way of thinking because it saves us the trouble of relearning everything each time we start a new day. But life is a constantly changing set of experiences, not a fixed pattern established by past events. The lessons of past experience can be very valuable, but they can lead us astray. A child who has been stung by a stinging nettle will know to avoid touching nettles in future, thus avoiding further pain. But a child who has fallen accidentally into a swimming pool may spend the rest of their life avoiding water, thus denying themselves a lot of potential pleasure.

We should be able to make the distinction between the lessons of one experience and another, but instead we get stuck in a fixed way of thinking. Because our thoughts tend towards negativity, this is a recipe for unhappiness.

And while your mind is preoccupied with problems, you ignore the pleasures in life. You can walk through a beautiful landscape, with sunlight dancing on the leaves of the trees, the grass glowing a vivid green, birds singing, insects buzzing, and drops of dew glinting like jewels on a spider's web, yet you see and hear none of it because your mind is preoccupied with pouncing on some imaginary pleasure or hiding from some imaginary pain.

You're not experiencing your reality; you're creating a false one in your mind. It's time to let go, stop struggling for control, and become a non-judgmental observer in your own experience.

FOURTH INSTRUCTION:
PAY ATTENTION TO YOUR POSITIVE EXPERIENCES
AS THEY OCCUR

EXERCISE: THE BODY SCAN

This simple exercise can be performed seated, walking, lying down, or standing up. If you choose to lie down and find yourself falling asleep, try a more upright position. But be mindful of your tiredness – it might be the case that sleep is the best thing you can do right now

For many people new to mindfulness, finding the time is one of the biggest challenges. This exercise requires just ten minutes. As you become more experienced, you can extend the body scan into more detail, right down to each finger and toe and the features of your face, but for beginners this version of the exercise will feel more accessible.

1. Bring yourself into a comfortable position. You can be seated on a chair with pillows supporting your back if necessary, lying down with your palms facing upwards, or standing. Make yourself as comfortable as possible. Relax your hands on your lap and close your eyes or softly focus on the floor in front of you.

2. First bring your attention to your breath, breathing in and out through your nose, following the natural rhythm of your breath. There is no need to force the breath, just follow it in and out, and feel the rise and fall of your belly as you breathe. As you relax, maintain an awareness of your body and the body part that you are focusing on. It can sometimes help to add a colour to the body part, or visualize it being illuminated.

3. Bring your attention to the crown of your head. The aim is not to change anything here; you're just focusing your attention. Now bring your attention steadily to your forehead, your left eye, your right eye, your right ear and the back of your head, your left ear and the left jaw, maybe consciously now placing a space between your teeth and resting and relaxing your tongue on the roof of your mouth. Focus on the right jaw, then the right side of the neck, then the back of the neck, and the left side of your neck, dropping your attention on to the left shoulder and the left arm, the upper arm, then lower arm, wrist, then hands, and then fingers on the left-hand side.

4. Now bring your awareness to the top of the chest, left chest, right chest, and the top of the back. Remember, you're not having to do anything, just bring your awareness to each body part. Move to the right shoulder and now focus on the right arm, upper arm,

lower arm, wrist, hand, and then the fingers on the right hand. Then bring your focus to your abdomen, your belly area and lower back, your pelvis and then your left hip. Now move it to the left leg, first the whole of the left leg, then the top of the leg, the left knee, lower leg, and ankle on the left-hand side. Rest your attention on your left foot and then your toes. Now bring your attention to the right hip and the whole of the right leg, the top of the leg, then the knee, the lower leg, ankle, right foot, and toes.

5. Now bring your attention back to the crown of your head, then sweep downward over the body parts and see if any area of the body is holding any tension or stress. If you are aware of any tension, try allowing these areas of tension to be held in your awareness. Nothing needs to be changed; just be present to them and hold them in your awareness.

6. When you're ready, slowly bring your attention to your fingers and toes, maybe bringing some movement into these areas, take a couple of good deep breaths, open your eyes, and finish with a stretch.

If you are performing this exercise for the first time you will almost certainly find your mind starting to wander.

Don't worry about it; just bring it gently back to the part of your body you were focusing on.

As you perform the body scan, test your ability to focus and refocus. When thoughts come into your mind, don't try to force them out, but see if you can gently refocus on the part of your body while you let the thought go. If you find yourself losing focus, return to the body part until you're ready to resume the scan. Try focusing in very closely on some parts and taking a broader view of others. Pay attention to any feelings that arise. If no feelings arise, be aware of the lack of feeling.

The body scan is a good way to begin to exercise awareness and develop your ability to focus your attention. The more you practise it, the easier it will become and you will be able to take it further.

SUMMARY

- **We are wired to focus on negatives but not to exaggerate them**

- **Worry becomes another big source of stress, creating a vicious circle**

- **Mindfulness recognizes problems without the pressure to solve them**

- **By letting go, you gain control**

- **Try to distinguish between the lessons of past experiences**

- **FOURTH INSTRUCTION: PAY ATTENTION TO YOUR POSITIVE EXPERIENCES AS THEY OCCUR**

CHAPTER 6
THE INCREDIBLE MACHINE

IN THIS CHAPTER
• REDISCOVER HOW TO USE YOUR SENSES • NATURE'S WARNING LIGHT
• SWEET NOTHING • THE THINGS YOU DON'T NOTICE

The body scan teaches us to pay attention to physical sensations. Perhaps you think that it's practically impossible to ignore physical sensations; feelings of pleasure or pain seldom go unnoticed. But if you follow the instructions for the body scan and have practised it, you will have realized that the way we normally respond to physical sensations is very superficial, even to the point of not really feeling at all.

It's not normal for us to focus on the feelings in different parts of our body. We are not, as a rule, taught to do it, and so we go through life without realizing that this ability is available to us. Instead, we make assumptions about our physical sensations and accept the opinions of so-called experts, who can only base their diagnoses on our vague descriptions of what we're feeling.

There are three pieces of brainwashing that lead us into the misery of depression, addiction, eating disorders, etc.:

1. The myth that the human mind and body are weak and need outside help in order to enjoy life and cope with stress.

2. The myth that drugs, junk food, etc., can compensate for these illusory weaknesses.

3. The myth that humans are more intelligent than the intelligence that created us, whatever you believe that to be.

REDISCOVER HOW TO USE YOUR SENSES

The belief that we are weak and incomplete creates our desire for some sort of crutch and we are brainwashed into believing that things like alcohol, nicotine, or sweets can provide that crutch. The illusion that these things then compensate for our weakness makes us dependent on them. It's a classic con trick, like selling a crutch riddled with woodworm to someone who hasn't got a broken leg.

The fact is we are much stronger and more capable than we realize. We show more respect for the man-made wonders of the industrial and technological revolutions than we do for the natural wonder that is humankind: we worship the car, the phone, the computer, for example. Without doubt, these are incredible machines. There is seemingly no limit to the functions a modern computer can perform in the blink of an eye, but spill a glass of wine over your keyboard and that incredible machine suddenly becomes rather useless.

That's not the case with your body. It too can perform millions of functions all at the same time without you even realizing and, while a glass of wine will slow it down and hamper your ability to carry out the more precise functions accurately, it won't cause an instant shutdown. What's more, some people pour wine into themselves for years and not only do they keep functioning, they don't even need to go in for repairs. They're the lucky ones. Not everyone is. But your body's ability to recover from the abuse you put it through is so remarkable that it puts any man-made machine to shame.

Your body is incredibly strong, and so are you. It is also incredibly sophisticated, capable of producing every drug and every instinctive reaction it needs to survive. It even boasts an early warning system designed to send you a clear signal when something is wrong. That signal is pain.

However, instead of regarding pain as a valuable survival tool, we treat it as an unnecessary evil and take drugs to anaesthetize it. That's like stopping your smoke alarm from sounding by unplugging it instead of finding the fire and putting it out. Much of the stress we suffer is brought about by striving to avoid pain.

NATURE'S WARNING LIGHT

Your car is not capable of repairing itself, but it can tell you when things are going wrong. For example, when the oil is running low, a light will come on to tell you so. When you see that light, you have three options.

1. Ignore it

2. Remove the bulb

3. Top up the engine oil.

Only one choice will prevent the engine from seizing up, but countless motorists have broken down as a result of taking one of the first two options, through laziness or a sense of "oh, it'll be all right for the time being".

Pain is nature's warning light and stupidly we tend to treat it the same way. We either ignore it until it becomes intolerable, by which time the problem has become severe, possibly even life-threatening, or we take painkillers. This is the same principle as removing the bulb. All it does is remove the symptom, not the cause. Yet we regard the pharmaceuticals industry as one of the great triumphs of human intellect, when all it has done is override our natural ability to protect ourselves from injury and disease.

If you regularly take painkillers for headaches, you're merely removing the bulb from the warning light. Wouldn't you rather remove whatever's causing the headaches?

Your senses are also part of that early warning system. Sight, smell, touch, and taste all play a part in detecting poison. Watch an animal approach food. First it will look at it from a safe distance, then it will go up and sniff it. It might prod the food with a paw and then, if all these senses are satisfied, it will taste it, tentatively at first.

You are equipped with the same senses and they do the same job for you. You can tell when an apple is rotten by looking at it. If it's just on the turn, it might look edible, but it will smell off and will be soft to the touch. If you took a bite, the taste would be repugnant and you would spit it out. An experience like that might put you off apples for a while. This is your body's way of protecting you from poison now and in the future, and it works when there are no role models or friends pressurizing you to persevere.

Your senses are trying to protect you when you first drink alcohol or smoke a cigarette. These things might be designed to look appealing, but the smell is your first warning. The taste is your second. That first taste of alcohol or cigarette smoke makes a lot of people gag. Some are actually sick. This is the next line of defence as your body does everything it can to expel the poison.

But budding smokers and drinkers are so taken with the belief that cigarettes and alcohol will give them some amazing pleasure or crutch that they keep putting themselves through this abuse. And all the while their body cleverly builds a tolerance against the poison until it no longer has the nauseous effect. They call this "acquiring the taste" but all they're acquiring is the loss of the sense of taste.

Ask anyone who has quit smoking and they will tell you that food tastes so much more interesting when you don't smoke. The fact is their body has recovered and they've regained the sense of taste.

Your perception of taste is hugely suggestible. The English showman chef Heston Blumenthal has played with this phenomenon by creating dishes in which the appearance and flavour are usually completely unassociated, such as bacon and egg ice cream. Not only is he offering a remarkable dining experience, he's also offering a sensory adventure. Eating a Heston Blumenthal dish forces you to think about the sensation in your mouth in a way that has become very alien to us.

Has anybody ever told you that cake is virtually tasteless, as are French fries, biscuits, cheese, meat, potatoes, and just about every other food that we commonly regard as our favourite? Or is this the first time that thought has crossed your mind? When you spend your life being bombarded with images of people apparently getting huge pleasure from eating these things, it's the natural intellectual response to believe it.

By following your intellectual response rather than paying attention to what your senses are telling you, you develop a false impression of those foods.

You might argue that it doesn't matter whether the food is really tasty or not – if you believe it tastes good, surely that's enough to give you pleasure from eating it. The trouble with this argument is that it leads us to eat all sorts of foods that are bad for us – and our inability to stop becomes a source of unhappiness. This is the principle by which most people in the developed world feed themselves. It's no coincidence that the developed world is also experiencing an epidemic of obesity and a sharp rise in cases of Type 2 diabetes as a result of poor diet.

There are plenty of people who stand to gain from keeping as many of us as possible trapped by this illusion of pleasure. Drugs companies, the tobacco and alcoholic drinks industries, the food industry, gambling firms… they've all become expert at exploiting our intellect to hoodwink us into making misguided, harmful choices.

The solution requires you to open your mind to the possibility that everything you've ever been told about the food you eat, the alcohol you drink, and the cigarettes you smoke is untrue.

Put your preconceptions to one side and start judging the facts for yourself.

SWEET NOTHING

Fruit is the food that nature designed us to eat above any other and our taste for the natural sugar in fruit is designed to keep us coming back for more. Refined sugar, packed into sweets, cakes, biscuits, and drinks, replicates the sweetness of fruit on our taste buds. It contains none of the goodness of fruit, but it tricks our taste buds into thinking it's the same thing. Through our intellect, we have created a substance that fools our instincts into thinking we are getting something good when, in truth, it's nothing but bad.

Next time you eat a confection or a cake, follow the instructions for mindful eating of a berry that you practised in Chapter One and really pay attention to the look, feel, smell, and taste of the food. Notice how the evidence from your senses compares to your assumptions about that food. Is there a difference?

When you practise mindful eating, you become adept at deciding for yourself which foods taste great, which taste bad, and which taste of very little at all. This makes it much easier to stop eating junk food.

Because of our intellect, we regard ourselves as superior to the rest of the animal kingdom, and with good reason: the inventions and creations of mankind are incredible even to us and way beyond the capabilities of the rest of the animal kingdom. Yet we also suffer in ways that are unique to us. You don't see wild animals destroying themselves with drug addictions or eating disorders, or torturing themselves with the accompanying bouts of self-loathing. Animals in their natural habitats do not overeat and are never obese. Don't misunderstand me – of course elephants and hippos are immense – but they are exactly the size they are supposed to be. All species demonstrate the same characteristic body shape. There are differences depending on age – but whatever species of animal you observe they're the same, fit, uniform body shape.

Unlike ourselves, animals don't commit their time to mutual destruction in the way we do.

The incredible human machine is flawed by placing intellect above instinct and allowing our experiences to be outmuscled by our thoughts. Our thoughts become our reality, a false impression at odds with actual experience that inevitably leads to unhappiness.

But the ability to think means we also have the ability to choose, so why do we so often take the self-destructive option? Quite simply,

WE DON'T ALWAYS REALIZE WE HAVE A CHOICE

NOTHING IS FIXED IN THE WAY YOU THINK

The practice of mindfulness teaches us to be present with our experiences. The assumption of a false reality that is created in your mind through brainwashing begins to give way to a knowledge of genuine reality perceived, not through thought, but through experience – the evidence of your senses.

You realize that there is a lot more to you than your thoughts.

When we allow thoughts to dominate our perception of reality, we divide our time between anxiety and regret – feeling anxious about the future and regretful about the past. This is not a recipe for happiness. And it is not reality.

Reality is what you experience yourself, via your senses. Senses only work in the present. You cannot see, hear, feel, taste, or smell things in the past or future. As you learn to pay attention to the evidence of your senses, it brings you into the present and you begin to shake off the assumptions that keep you trapped in the cycle of misery.

The real benefit of this is that you stop seeing problems as part of yourself and start observing them objectively for what they really are. For example, rather than thinking, "I've got backache," and giving yourself that label, you observe the sensation as a temporary sensation: "There is a pain in my back right now."

Now you can recognize that your physical sensations are not permanent; they are constantly changing. You are no longer stuck with a false assumption that gets you down and, by freeing yourself from that depressing assumption, you will feel a sense of relief.

THE THINGS YOU DON'T NOTICE

The body scan teaches us to be present with our physical experiences and we learn to notice sensations that previously went unobserved. If there are so many sensations constantly taking place in your own body without you noticing, imagine how much is happening in the world around you that goes unobserved.

You don't have to imagine; you simply have to use your senses. Open your eyes to the colours in a sunset, the light catching the leaves, a spider spinning a web. Listen to the sound of the birds, the insects, the fingers of your colleague tapping on a keyboard. Sniff the air. Is it fresh? If not, what can you smell? How does it make you feel?

Practise connecting with your senses as you go about your everyday business and pay attention to how it affects your perception of the world around you. Rather than letting your mind wander into thoughts about the future or past, focus your attention on what's going on in the present.

It might feel a little strange at first, but what we're asking you to do is not hard. If you find your mind wandering back into thought, just acknowledge the fact without judgment and bring your focus gently back to the present. With practice, you will find that you get better at maintaining your attention in the present.

The human body is an incredible machine controlled by an incredible computer – the mind.

The development of awareness is like being given the handbook to your own mind: you begin to see how it really works; you begin to observe your own thought processes. And the realization that you can observe your own thoughts releases you from the fixed belief that you *are* your thoughts. This is incredibly liberating.

All that's really happened is that you've been made aware that you have a choice. That awareness enables you to make full use of the incredible machine. With practice, the ability to observe when you are getting caught up in negative thoughts and gently move your focus back to the present becomes second nature.

In fact, it's first nature.

Awareness is the facility we have lost by placing intellect above instinct and becoming stuck with false assumptions. We *think* our way through life without stopping to *feel* what's really happening to us. Awareness is the key to unlock the full potential of the incredible human machine – the potential for

HAPPINESS

SUMMARY

- False assumptions lead us to make harmful choices

- We are stronger and more capable than we are led to believe

- A lot of bad choices are down to not realizing you have a choice

- Practise being present with your experiences

- Awareness proves there is more to you than your thoughts

- Awareness is the key to happiness

CHAPTER 7
HOW MINDFULNESS CAN HELP

IN THIS CHAPTER
• FREEING YOUR MIND • CHOOSING HAPPINESS
• PROVEN HEALTH BENEFITS • THE COUNTERCLOCKWISE EXPERIMENT
• YOU HAVE THE POWER • EXERCISE: COUNTING THE BREATH

We live in a world full of pressures. We have established that the stress we feel is a combination of anxiety and regret – anxiety about things that lie in the future, regret about things that happened in the past. Our anxiety and regret are fuelled by thoughts put into our heads by brainwashing, which causes us to hold on to fixed ideas.

When our minds wander, they tend towards negativity, even though we have more positive experiences in life than negative ones. But our fixed ideas of negativity prevent us from seeing things as they really are. We might tell ourselves "I have a bad leg", or "I am old", or "I can't get a job". We have a desire for certainty, which leads us to imagine things as fixed, permanent conditions that cannot and will not be changed.

Mindfulness helps us to see the true picture: that everything in life is constantly changing; nothing is permanent and, therefore, everything can be changed for the better. This has the potential to immediately put us in a more upbeat, positive frame of mind, and that positivity gives us the momentum to effect change for the better.

The body scan is a gentle way of practising mindfulness and the more you practise it, the easier it becomes. The benefits are many:

FREEING YOUR MIND

Paying attention to the sensations in the body scan makes you aware that things are constantly changing. You notice how stress rises and falls and how your mind wandering to different places causes that rise and fall. As a result, you become aware of those fixed ideas that cause stress and unhappiness, and can let them go.

SEEING THE JOY

The body scan teaches you to appreciate the miraculous workings of the human body – things most of us take for granted – and by extension you start to feel a greater sense of appreciation of the wonders of the world you live in. This leads to a greater joy being derived from the real things in life, like the sunrise, birdsong, fresh grass, etc., which creates a more positive, appreciative mindset.

ACCEPTANCE

Gentleness and non-judgment are key aspects of mindfulness and they require a different approach to the one most of us are conditioned to have. As you practise the body scan, you learn to observe pleasure and pain with the same approach – not trying to cling on to them or fix them but simply accepting their presence. Being kind to yourself, accepting your own tendency to wander, rather than punishing yourself for it, takes the stress out of the practice and gives you the breathing space to improve without unnecessary pressure.

OPENING YOUR MIND

Paying attention to the workings of your own mind paves the way to becoming more proficient at accepting negativity, not getting hooked up into it, but steering away from it towards happiness. You notice how your mind has the tendency to wander all the time, which helps to unravel the assumption that you have control over your thoughts. By opening your mind to your own susceptibility to distraction, you can then begin to practise and improve your ability to bring your attention back to focus.

SENSING RATHER THAN THINKING

The focusing of attention on your body begins the process of coming out of your head and reconnecting with your senses. In so doing, you start to experience reality in the present, through what you actually feel, rather than basing your experience on thoughts and beliefs, which tend to occupy the past or the future.

LEANING INTO DISCOMFORT

The normal response to unpleasant feelings is to try to get rid of them, either by grappling with them, trying to think of a solution, or pretending they don't exist. This creates a stressed mindset that makes the unpleasant feelings worse. The mindful approach in the body scan teaches you not to avoid or avert discomfort but to approach it with gentle interest and to take in the full picture of that discomfort, be it physical pain or unpleasant emotions. This may not make the discomfort go away, but it does avoid adding that extra layer of stress caused by agonizing about it.

LEARNING TO PAY ATTENTION

The idea that the brain can be retrained is one that we tend to be closed to until we try it. Expressions like "You can't teach an old dog new tricks" leave the impression that your mind is formed as a child and there is no changing it in adulthood. This has been comprehensively disproven by scientific research. Just like your body, the brain can be tuned, honed, and strengthened in very specific ways through certain types of mental exercise. Unlike gym work, the exercise is gentle, relaxed but ultimately every bit as rewarding. The more you train your mind to focus on one part of the body, then move on to another, the easier it becomes. From the initial attempts when your mind wanders repeatedly, you soon develop a much greater ability to pay attention and direct your attention wherever you want.

CHOOSING HAPPINESS

The body scan is a great way to see – in many cases for the first time – the incredible power of your consciousness, and of your awareness. As you begin to develop the ability to place your attention exactly where you want it, the power of now, the power of the present, of awareness, of the mind to follow that instruction, and the sensations you become aware of as a result are a revelation.

When you are well practised at mindfulness, you will find you have a greater attention span. You will also have the ability to extract yourself from negative assumptions and place your attention on more positive experiences, which means you can feel more in control, and actively direct your mind towards peace and happiness.

I have explained how and why the human mind has a tendency to wander towards negative thoughts. With mindfulness training, you become aware of the wandering and that awareness gives you the power to do something about it.

Think back to the box of flies analogy. When you're not mindful, it feels like you're in the box, plagued by the flies buzzing around your head. Through mindfulness, you can extract yourself from the box, observe the flies from a disconnected perspective, and make a conscious decision to move your consciousness to a less stressful environment.

PROVEN HEALTH BENEFITS

Scientific research has revealed some extraordinary health benefits due to the practice of mindfulness. In addition to the increased ability to stay focused as mentioned above, it has been shown to improve the following mental faculties:

- Memory and recall

- Processing information

- Problem solving

- Cognitive skills

- Creativity

- Decision-making.

The effect on emotional wellbeing has also been shown to be profound, with benefits including:

- Reduced stress levels

- Reduced fear and anxiety

- Reduced depression

- Reduced sense of loneliness

- Heightened sense of optimism

- Enhanced self-esteem

- Greater resilience

- Greater social confidence

- Heightened emotional intelligence

- Lessened impulsiveness

• Reduction in phobias.

Arguably the most extraordinary benefits of mindfulness are those that have been shown to occur in the body:

• Reduced blood pressure

• Improved breathing

• Heightened energy levels

• Bolstered immune system

• Reduced heart rate

• Improved mobility

• Enhanced eyesight

• Improved hearing

• Greater dexterity

• Reduced pain from arthritis.

THE COUNTERCLOCKWISE EXPERIMENT

In 1979, a Harvard psychologist called Ellen Langer embarked on an experiment to see if the effects of ageing could be altered by changing thought patterns. Her methodology was to take two groups of elderly men, in their late 70s and 80s, to a retreat in Massachusetts and subject them to a "week of reminiscence", in which their focus would be taken back 20 years to 1959.

The first group were encouraged to reminisce about their lives in the 1950s; the second group were immersed in an environment that replicated 1959 in every possible detail. The retreat was decorated and furnished in late 50s style; the men were shown films, played music, and exposed to the news items of the time.

At the same time these infirm, elderly men were encouraged to fend for themselves as they would have done when 20 years younger. They were left to carry their own suitcases and take care of their own day-to-day needs without assistance. In short, they were treated as healthy individuals, not as incompetent or sick.

The results were remarkable. Not only did they cope with cooking their own meals and other household chores, Langer also noticed that they started walking faster, moving, and acting more confidently, and making their own decisions. One man, who had come in with the aid of a stick, threw the stick away and joined in a game of catch!

Being a good scientist, Langer took measurements at the beginning and end of the experiment to prove the physiological changes. The measurements showed an all-round improvement in the way the men walked, their manual dexterity, speed, cognitive abilities, and memory. They also showed a fall in blood pressure, enhanced appetite, and reduced arthritic pain. Most extraordinary of all – because these are two things that general wisdom holds to be irreversible – their hearing and eyesight improved.

These improvements were evident in both groups but were more pronounced in the second group, the one that had been immersed in the world of 1959. The conclusion is powerful: by freeing the mind from fixed ideas of oneself and one's own abilities, we can effect positive physiological changes. In other words, by unsticking the mind from assumptions of infirmity, weakness, inability, hopelessness, etc., and moving our focus towards good health, strength, dexterity, and hope, we begin to recover our health.

Since Ellen Langer's experiment in 1979, further research has shown the positive effects of mindfulness in a wide range of important applications. It has been shown to improve people's ability to process pain and increase their ability to regulate pain, thus reducing it. A similar effect has been found in the control of stress. The effect of mindfulness practice on the brain has been measured and found to strengthen areas associated with stress regulation.

We are all familiar with expressions like "Look before you leap", "Think before you speak", "Take a deep breath", etc., all aimed at encouraging a less impulsive, calmer level of behaviour. What we're actually encouraging with these remarks is mindfulness. Children who have been schooled in paying attention and being aware of their thoughts have been shown to be less impulsive in their behaviour. Other experiments have shown that mindfulness can have a positive effect on ADHD.

People with phobias are also encouraged to breathe when faced with their fear. Whether it's spiders, heights, confined spaces, or any of the many other so-called "irrational fears" that millions of people live with, regulating your breathing is proven to help reduce the physical effects of fear, though it doesn't take away the fear itself.

Through mindfulness, people with phobias are encouraged to focus on their fear rather than trying to put it out of their mind and, as a result, their level of fear is reduced.

The mindful approach to cravings and addictions, as evidenced by the success of Allen Carr's Easyway, has been shown to be the most effective method for quitting smoking, drinking, and other addictions, not only in terms of the ease with which people quit but the fact that they stay stopped and, equally importantly, that they enjoy life more when they are free.

I see the evidence of how effective a mindful approach is to quitting smoking, drinking, gambling, etc., on a daily basis. Quite simply, when you pay attention to your addiction and develop awareness of what it really does for you – i.e. absolutely nothing – you remove any reason, and thus any desire, to continue. Easyway has shown millions of people that they have a choice they never realized they had – the choice to be happy. It has been shown that the wandering mind tends towards unhappiness. Easyway shows you how to train your mind away from the negative assumptions put into your mind through brainwashing and towards appreciating the many wonderful things in life.

YOU HAVE THE POWER

The beauty of the Easyway method, and of mindfulness in general, is that it is not something you have to acquire or achieve, it is something you merely have to access. That's why it's called Easyway – because there is no hardship involved. All you have to do is open your mind and follow a set of simple instructions.

EXERCISE: COUNTING THE BREATH

When learning the principles of mindfulness, there is sometimes a perception that it is about banishing thoughts. This is not the case. Your brain will always produce thoughts – thinking is one of the brain's key functions. It's important that you don't get the impression that thinking is a problem. Thinking is an incredible faculty and it has innumerable benefits. What matters is that you don't allow thoughts to dominate your senses and thus create a false perception of reality. The ability to detach yourself from thoughts when you want to and to refocus your mind when it wanders is a skill that can help you greatly reduce stress and anxiety.

For example, as soon as you close your eyes, you may have a thought that you are hungry. That's fine. If, though, you find your mind wandering to your fridge, working out what you will be eating later, then it's time to bring it back to the present. Counting the breath is a very good way to train the mind to focus on one thing.

This exercise can be done seated, lying down, standing, or walking. Before you begin, place a hand on the top of your chest and the other on your stomach and see which hand rises when you breathe. If it's the top hand, then try to encourage the breath to come from lower down, from your belly. Shallow breathing – breathing from the chest – is a sign of anxiety. Tellingly, it is where most people breathe from.

If you are seated, try to have your feet firmly on the floor, feeling the meeting point of floor and feet, your back straight, supported with cushions if required, and hands resting and relaxed in the lap.

Set a timer for an amount of time you feel comfortable with but at least five minutes. Begin by taking a few deep breaths, right down into your belly, and then allowing your body to naturally breathe for you. As you breathe, begin to follow the natural rhythm of your breath, trying not to force your breath, just following it. Feel the sensation of the cool air in your nostrils as you breathe in and out through your nose, and as you bring your attention to the sensation of the breath begin counting the breaths.

Begin to count the "in" breath as 1 and the "out" breath as 2, the next "in" breath as 3 and the "out" breath as 4. Keep counting up to 10 and then go back to 1. As thoughts, emotions and feelings begin to arise, bring yourself back to 1, back to counting the breath, so allowing those thoughts and feelings to arise and pass, just observing, relaxing, and breathing.

There is so little to do here: just count and breathe… back to 1. If you find yourself counting over 10, just bring yourself back to 1, with kindness, back to 1. After a while you may find that you are able to drop counting the "in" breath and you can just count the "out" breath – whatever is comfortable for you, just counting and breathing and letting thoughts arise and pass.

When you are ready, softly open your eyes and have a stretch.

With time and practice, you will begin to realize that you are not your thoughts – that they are not who you are. A good analogy is to imagine your thoughts as boats on a river. As you follow your breath, you are sitting on the riverbank watching the boats go by. Sometimes the river is very busy and sometimes it's very quiet, but that is never the point – the point is, you are observing the river, regardless of the weight of traffic. If you find you have been pulled in by one of the boats, then you come back gently and kindly to the riverbank – back to the breath, back to observing.

The point about kindness is that you place no pressure on yourself to do the exercise well or criticise yourself for losing focus. It is not a case of being good or bad, only a question of whether you were present or not. Even to admit you weren't present is recognition that you were doing the exercise. Let the thought go and return to the breath.

SUMMARY

- Everything is constantly changing and, therefore, can be changed for the better

- You have the power to focus on happiness

- Mindfulness is not just a method for tackling stress; it has proven physical benefits too

- Focus your mind on positive thoughts and your body will respond accordingly

CHAPTER 8
FIRST STEPS TO HAPPINESS

IN THIS CHAPTER
• SEEING THE PROBLEM • CHANGING YOUR MINDSET
• RECOGNIZING THE TOOLS AVAILABLE TO YOU • PRACTICE MAKES PERFECT

The second instruction was "BEGIN WITH A FEELING OF ELATION". Perhaps you think that's too simplistic. If you could choose to feel elated whenever you wanted, surely you would never be unhappy.

Here's some good news for you:

YOU CAN!

All you need is to see that you have a choice.

SEEING THE PROBLEM

When your head is stuck in the box of flies, it's very hard to see that there might be a better way to solve the problem that doesn't involve hitting out at the flies. So your life becomes a series of knee-jerk reactions, flailing about as you try to cling on to pleasure and push away pain. We add to our stress by trying to fix things in our minds. We wrack our brains to right wrongs, avert problems, prolong pleasures, restore damages, change outcomes... The mental torment keeps us awake at night and never leads to resolution. In fact, it makes matters worse, by adding stress and tiredness to the anxiety.

But you keep pursuing this way of thinking because it's the only way you know. You're so caught up in the box of flies that it never crosses your mind that the way to stop the buzzing might be to stop fighting, stop avoiding, stop trying to think of solutions.

You become stuck in a fixed approach to both pleasure and displeasure, which only causes anxiety – a fear that pleasures will be lost and that displeasures will hurt you. This is all thought; it is not experience. By filling your mind with fixed ideas, perceptions, and assumptions, you fall out of step with experience. Real life moves on and you get left behind.

With your mind fixed on your anxieties, you become blind to reality. You miss the good things that are actually happening in life and instead become stuck in sadness or depression. So what do you do to try and relieve the misery? You turn to external sources: alcohol, nicotine, other drugs, spending, eating, gambling… The trap has claimed another victim. You have been brainwashed into thinking you can make yourself happy by doing something that is harmful. In fact, you know it is harmful, but the brainwashing is so thorough that the belief becomes firmly fixed in your mind. And when the drugs, or the junk food, or whatever don't bring you the pleasure you were hoping for, rather than seeing that they don't work and quitting, you assume you haven't gone far enough and take more!

It's essential that you realize the unshakeable truth about drugs, junk food, and all the other so-called 'crutches':

DRUGS DO NOT HELP – THEY MAKE MATTERS WORSE

As long as you continue to believe that you can get happy by smoking, drinking, etc., you will remain in the trap. Release can be as simple as being told that you have a choice. All you need to do is open your mind to the possibility that this is true and follow a simple instruction. You don't even have to believe in the instruction – just by following it, you will discover the proof for yourself.

You have every reason to feel elated. You are being given the key to freedom from stress and misery. All you have to do is keep following the instructions and the key will work for you. This is a marvellous moment, a life-changing moment.

Imagine you really are a prisoner, kept in a dark, miserable cell for years. Then one day someone comes and tells you they have the key for you to escape. Would you wait until you were out of the prison before you felt elated? Or would you feel the elation as soon as you knew escape was within your grasp?

That's how you should feel now. Escape is within your grasp and you already have the key. All you have to do is use it.

CHANGING YOUR MINDSET

When you hold on to the belief that life is desperate and hard, misery becomes part of your self-image and you behave accordingly. "Smile? What is there to smile about?"

With your head stuck in the box of flies, it's very hard to see anything to smile about. When you lift your head out of the box and become aware of everything that's happening around you, you realize there is no shortage of things to smile about.

The human mind is so incredible, though, that even when you're plagued by the constant buzz of pressure and anxiety, you can still be aware that this is all symptomatic of a bigger problem that requires help.

You may not see the solution, but the very awareness that there is a problem is enough to steer you on to a different path. The fact that you're reading this book is evidence that you are aware of the need for help. Your anxieties may be all-consuming, but your mind still has the capacity to make you aware that there is a bigger problem.

It's also true, however, that we have a tendency to push big problems to the back of our minds and bury them there. We do this because we're afraid that we will have to go through some traumatic challenge in order to solve them. Rest assured, there is no trauma with Easyway.

The key is to open your mind and let go of those fixed ideas. As you open your mind and let go of your assumptions, you become aware of the full capability of the mind. You begin to observe your thoughts from a more detached perspective, allowing them to pass across your mind without feeling the need to cling on to them or hide away from them.

In the last exercise, counting the breath, you were introduced to the practice of bringing your thoughts back to focus on the breath whenever they begin to wander. In doing so, you learn to access much more of the power of your consciousness than you do when you're merely absorbed in thought. It's like being the shepherd rather than the sheep.

You learn to be aware of your thoughts and to shepherd them with a kind, non-judgmental attitude, putting them wherever you want them. The fact that you are now observing your thoughts, rather than being surrounded by them, proves that there is a level in your mind above thought. Therefore, there is more to you than your thoughts.

With practice, you will become more and more adept at shepherding your wandering thoughts back to the point of focus. As you practise the body scan, you will experience a closer connection with your own physical reality, becoming acutely aware of what you're really feeling in your joints, muscles, organs, etc., as you pay attention to your senses.

As you connect more deeply with your senses, you develop a richer appreciation of everyday pleasures like eating, nature, and relaxation. When you pay attention to the everyday pleasures, you realize that there is plenty to smile about. You notice that there is never nothing going on – there is always something to remind you of the miracle of your own existence, the incredible machine that you own, and the extraordinary planet you live on.

When you're wrapped up in negative thoughts, these natural wonders lose their shine. You see only the problems. The reality hasn't changed – only your mindset. Planet Earth is still an extraordinary place, the human body is still an incredible machine, and life is still an intricate collection of miracles. The only reason for not seeing it that way is that your mind has become dominated by negativity.

You weren't born that way. And you don't have to stay that way. The fourth instruction was to pay attention to positive experiences. Too often we move through life focusing on false pleasures and missing the genuine pleasures that are happening around us all the time.

All you need to do is change your mindset. Tell yourself to

pay attention and you will – it's as simple as that. And when you pay attention, you will notice things that change your mindset away from negative thinking. By following one simple instruction, you can trigger a cycle of awareness and positivity that becomes self-perpetuating.

RECOGNIZING THE TOOLS AVAILABLE TO YOU

It's a revelation when you realize you have a choice to be happy. It marks the beginning of an awakening of your mind to the full power of the incredible machine. And all it takes is someone to point it out to you.

That was what Easyway did for smokers that no one had done before: it told them they could quit easily, without willpower, and without the need for a painful withdrawal period, and it gave them a simple set of instructions to do so. There was no magic involved, no secret formula. It was pure common sense. But for smokers who quit with Easyway, it was a revelation.

THEY HAD NEVER THOUGHT TO THINK THAT WAY

And that's the problem. We get stuck in one way of thinking and become blind to reality. As you change your mindset you begin to realize you have powers that you were not aware of.

There is nothing mystical about this. It's not hocus-pocus or mind control or anything at all peculiar. On the contrary, it's the most natural thing in the world. All you are doing is accessing the full power of awareness, the power of your consciousness and body.

Doesn't it seem incredible that we all have a computer as powerful as the human brain yet most of us have no idea how to use it? Indeed, we regard anything that helps us to access that power with suspicion. We are brainwashed into perceiving mindfulness as "weird", and so we avoid it, rather than taking an open-minded approach to find out for ourselves whether it can help or not. We sleepwalk through life denying the full potential of our minds to help us see things as they really are.

Fear makes us shut down certain mental functions. We try to avoid threats. We hide from displeasure. But it's a sure way to make matters worse. Problems are allowed to grow and we can't close our minds to the fact that they're nagging away at us, so our anxiety builds, we hide more, and turn to false pleasures for relief. Now we have another problem: addiction to those false pleasures. And so the cycle continues and we become more and more disconnected from our ability to be happy.

The problem with clinging to pleasures and hiding from displeasures is that both actions create an inaccurate picture of experience. In simple terms, we develop the fear that any pleasure is something we can't live without and any pain is something we can't live with. As a result, both pleasure and pain make us anxious.

With mindfulness, you learn to keep both pleasure and pain in perspective by observing them from a more detached standpoint. This lessens any fear associated with them. Instead of giving yourself anxiety and false assumptions, you are able to focus on the experience and see it for what it really is – an experience that is happening to you, not a fixed part of you. By recognizing the changeability of a sensation, whether it's positive or negative, you become less attached to it and, therefore, more able to let it go. It's when we can't let go that we become anxious.

PRACTICE MAKES PERFECT

The language of mindfulness can sometimes leave people feeling alienated. The word itself is often perceived as meaning something mystical, wrapped up in Buddhist philosophy, meditation, and vows of silence. In fact, it is not mystical at all – on the contrary, it's very straightforward. It is exactly what we were given the tools to do.

You could substitute mindfulness with other terms, such as awareness, paying attention, noticing, or being present. Just as children are taught to pay attention in school, mindfulness teaches us to pay attention in life. It doesn't require any special powers – you already have the powers; all you need to do is practise using them.

When talking about mindfulness we use expressions like "letting go"; "detaching yourself from your thoughts", "seeing things as they really are"; and "choosing happiness". These might sound like abstract concepts and as long as they remain concepts – ideas with a fixed identity in your mind – they will continue to appear abstract and impracticable.

But as soon as you try putting them into practice, they begin to take form and you quickly see what they mean and how they work.

This is why opening your mind is so important. As long as you have a mental resistance to an idea that prevents you from following it, that idea will always remain abstract. Open your mind and follow the instructions and you will have an experience that changes your mindset.

As you practise the mindfulness exercises in this book and follow all the instructions, you will find yourself becoming more adept at focusing your mind on positive thoughts. It's like any other form of physical exercise – the more you do it, the easier it becomes and the better you become at doing it.

So if you're still finding your mind wandering when you're doing the body scan or counting the breath, there is no need to worry. Remember to take an attitude of gentleness and curiosity. You can't be expected to master it overnight.

But the change in your mindset can happen straight away. Just by turning your mind towards new ideas you open it up to revelations.

Your senses are working all the time and you will notice this as soon as you pay attention to them. If you followed the mindful berry eating exercise in Chapter One (and if you didn't, please do it now), you will have been aware of the vast amount of detail that we normally ignore when we eat. Simply by turning your mind towards that detail, you will see that there is a world of experience happening all the time, just waiting to be noticed.

SUMMARY

- **Remember, YOU HAVE A CHOICE**

- **Follow all the instructions and the proof will become evident**

- **You don't have to wait to feel elated**

- **Be the shepherd of your thoughts**

- **Tell yourself to pay attention**

- **Open your mind to its full potential**

- **Keep both pleasure and pain in perspective**

- **Practice makes perfect**

CHAPTER 9
FEAR

IN THIS CHAPTER
• A LIFESAVER • HOW FEAR AFFECTS US
• THE ADDICT'S TUG-OF-WAR • REAL VS IMAGINARY FEAR

The incredible machine that is the human body is equipped with myriad sophisticated functions that keep you alive from day to day. There are functions that tell you when to find food, when to sleep, when to move, when to blink… Without you even having to think, your body carries out countless complex processes every second, all of which are designed to keep you alive and functioning.

A LIFESAVER

We can philosophize about the meaning of life and our purpose on this planet, but when you examine the functions of the incredible machine, it's clear that it was designed for one purpose:

SURVIVAL

For our ancestors, the five senses were their key to survival. They detected threats in a number of ways: for example, the roar of a lion, the taste of poison, the heat of fire, the sight of a predator, and the smell of smoke. In primitive times, our senses were our early warning system, telling us about the threat of danger.

And how did our ancestors respond when danger was present? With fear.

Fear is the function that triggers a response to danger. It causes us to react in one of three ways: fight, flight, or freeze. The first two are probably familiar to you. The "fight or flight" response is well researched and documented. When triggered by fear, the body rapidly produces hormones that enhance your ability to either run away or engage in physical combat. These hormones heighten your senses and make you stronger, faster, and more aggressive.

Before the fight or flight responses kick in, though, there is a split second in which you freeze. You could call it surprise. It's the moment when you make your decision to run away, or stand your ground and fight. In this moment, your eyes widen, your hearing sharpens, and your mind works rapidly to assess the situation.

But the freeze moment doesn't always pass. You might judge that it's too late to run and you will stand no chance in a fight. The freeze response becomes your last resort. It is, in effect, designed to make you non-existent in the eyes of a predator. It is the response that says "hide!" or "play dead!"

Like a rabbit caught in the headlights, we hold our breath and hope the danger will pass, not noticing us or deciding we're not worth bothering with. If you've ever been frightened by noises in the night, you will probably have behaved in the same way. Pull the bedclothes up over your face, lie as still and quiet as possible, and listen intently for further evidence of what danger you're in.

HOW FEAR AFFECTS US

We talk about being paralyzed by fear. The freeze response does exactly that. It shuts you down, brings everything to a stop. In extreme cases, you become incapable of moving, even when you know it's your only option.

Think of somebody on a high ledge terrified by the drop beneath them. Frightened to move a muscle in case it causes them to lose their footing and fall, they remain rooted to the spot, literally paralyzed with fear. They know they can't stay on that ledge forever, but no amount of coaxing and reassurance will free them from the paralysis and get them to move off the ledge on their own. It usually takes a helicopter and a hoist to get them down.

The freeze response can become a permanent state of mind if the perceived danger never goes away. Anxiety takes hold and becomes your everyday condition. You begin to see yourself as an anxious person, rather than a person experiencing some anxiety.

As well as shutting down your physical functions, it closes your mind. Fear makes you less inclined to try new things. Even though you know that your present condition is causing you harm, you feel more comfortable with "the Devil you know" than you do with alternatives.

The freeze response is what lies behind the tendency for hiding and avoidance. Commonly known as "burying your head in the sand", hiding and avoidance are not a logical response but a desperate last measure when all other options have run out.

That might be understandable for a rabbit cornered by a fox but for a human being worried about the number of emails they get, it's clearly not the most logical response. Once again it's important to remember:

YOU DO HAVE A CHOICE!

That is not to dismiss the anxiety that we feel from the stresses of modern life. The pressure of work, money, relationships, social occasions, etc., can be terrifying and statistics show that more and more people are suffering with the effects of the anxiety it causes. High blood pressure, skin conditions, respiratory problems, digestive issues, heart palpitations, and sleep deprivation are all symptoms of fear when it sets in as an ongoing condition. Along with the physical symptoms come the mental conditions of sadness and depression. These mental and physical symptoms can trigger each other off, creating a vicious circle of misery and illness.

This vicious circle is easy to stop and reverse but only if you follow the right method. It's often as simple as seeing your situation from an objective point of view and recognizing that it's nowhere near as serious as your mind has led you to believe. The trouble is, we don't look to our own minds for the solution. We are brainwashed into seeking relief from our fears through other means: most commonly alcohol, nicotine, and other drugs.

Social occasions will often make us feel low on confidence. "Will I know anyone there?"; "Will they find me interesting?"; "Will I meet anyone I like?" Whatever happened to unpredictability! Nevertheless, these questions raise fears within us, and so we reach for a drink to quell those fears. We have been brainwashed into believing two myths about booze:

1. It gives you courage.

2. That losing inhibitions helps you.

Let's look at the first one first. The term "Dutch courage" originates from the days when English troops were given Dutch gin to calm their nerves before going into battle. There's an important distinction here: it may well have calmed their nerves by knocking out those particular emotions, but it didn't *give* them anything else, least of all courage.

Courage is acting in spite of fear. A fireman who runs into a burning building to rescue a baby is not fearless – he knows only too well the danger he is in and any fully conscious human who is in danger will feel fear. Yet he sets the fear for his own life aside to save the life of the baby. That is true courage.

If you knock out fear with alcohol, you leave yourself vulnerable to danger.

It is a mistake to regard fear as debilitating. As the above example shows, it is the absence of fear that is debilitating. There is nothing genuinely frightening about a social occasion, but there are dangers associated with them, such as getting home in one piece and, for women in particular, making sure you don't leave yourself vulnerable.

When we are in real danger, we need all our faculties to be fully functional: the ability to run, to shout, to fight, to think. Fear triggers all these responses. Knock out fear with alcohol and you are effectively burying your head in the sand. The effect is two-fold: you not only fail to identify danger when it arises; you also lack the ability to respond.

THE ADDICT'S TUG-OF-WAR

When you put your faith in a substance like alcohol to help you overcome your fear, addiction takes hold and you find yourself in a tug-of-war between two contrary fears: the fear of the harm that drinking is doing to you and the fear of what might happen if you try to quit.

Drinkers, smokers, other drug addicts, gamblers, overeaters, and overspenders are all well aware of the risk they're running, but, brainwashed into believing that they derive some pleasure or support from their little crutch, they fear life without it. So they make excuses that enable them to carry on because they are afraid of what might happen if they try to quit

Fear is the basis of all addiction. It is the force that makes the trap so ingenious, convincing the addict that they are deriving some form of pleasure or crutch. It is ingenious because it works back to front. It's when you are not getting your fix that you suffer the empty, insecure feeling. When you get your fix, you feel a small boost, which partially relieves the insecurity and your brain is fooled into believing that the fix is giving you a boost. In fact, it created the fear in the first place. The more you indulge in your little crutch, the more it drags you down and the greater your dependency on it.

This is why addicts can never win while they're in the trap. When you're getting your fix, you wish you didn't have to. It's only when you can't get it that it appears to be precious. You mope for something that doesn't exist, a subconscious illusion: the perception of a pleasure or crutch.

Many smokers, when asked why they don't quit, reply that they're afraid they won't be able to. The fear of failure holds them back.

Think about that logically. If you try to quit, what is the worst that can happen? You fail and remain a smoker. If you don't try, you GUARANTEE that you remain a smoker. Choosing to remain a smoker because of the fear of failure is illogical. You are, in effect, fearing a calamity that has already happened: you *are* a smoker!

The fear of failure can be put to good use. The physical responses can help an actor to remember their lines and inject energy into their performance, or an athlete to run faster and for longer. In fact, we can all use the fear of failure to help us succeed. It is no excuse for not trying.

There is a more complex fear that holds back addicts who want to quit:

THE FEAR OF SUCCESS

Why would anyone fear success? It could only be because you have a negative perception of what success looks like. For many addicts, quitting suggests a lifetime of deprivation and misery. They have been brainwashed into believing they will be making a terrible sacrifice. Without their little crutch, life will be full of insecurity and they'll never be able to enjoy living in the way they do now.

As any non-addict can tell them, life without addiction is infinitely better. You suffer less stress; you are better able to handle setbacks; you have more energy; you become more relaxed and happy; you value yourself more highly; you cope better in social situations... The list goes on.

It's not just people with recognized addictions who feel the fear of success and the fear of failure. Anyone who feels the need to make a life change will experience these fears in some measure. The key is to recognize that they are not rational fears; they are fears based on imagination, illusions, and brainwashing. You can do this by paying attention to your emotions in a mindful way and seeing them for what they are, rather than allowing them to trigger the freeze response.

REAL VS IMAGINARY FEAR

For humans, fear is both an instinctive and an intellectual response. Our intellect has enabled us to learn about potential dangers and how to avoid them, but the consequences that make us fearful can be both real and imaginary.

There are many things in modern life that can drive us into a panic:

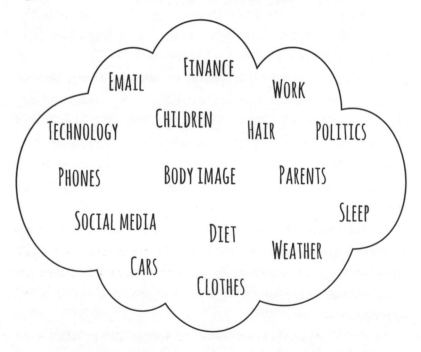

When you're already stressed, any little threat can trigger fear symptoms: a bad hair day when you've got a date or a job interview; a friend behaving moodily for no apparent reason; the children asking for money that you don't have...

All these things can trigger a typical fear response, whether it's running away from the problem, trying to fight it away, or letting it paralyze us into inertia, and hoping it will disappear.

It's easy to see how any of these responses can – and usually do – make the problem worse. By either overreacting or underreacting we fail to put the problem in perspective and deal with it calmly and effectively. We put ourselves under unnecessary stress, sour relationships with friends and family, beat ourselves up, make ourselves tired and ill, and take on the mantle of someone struggling to cope.

All this because of a situation that poses absolutely no threat to our survival. Running away from a lion is an entirely reasonable response.

Running away from a full email inbox is not. Yet, the anxiety a full email box can cause is very real to those who suffer it. As long as you remain trapped in your fear, you will not be able to see it for what it really is.

If we are to turn back the wave of stress and anxiety caused by all these aspects of modern life and make happiness our default emotion, it's essential that we learn to discern the difference between real and imaginary threats and then respond to them appropriately.

In order to do that, we need to follow the principles of mindfulness and examine our fears in detail.

SUMMARY

- Fear is not a problem; it's the key to our survival

- It becomes a problem when it makes you close your mind

- Smoking, alcohol, comfort eating, etc., only add to the problem

- Learn to distinguish between real and imaginary fears

- Most modern fears are imaginary

CHAPTER 10
ACCEPTING FEAR THROUGH MINDFULNESS

IN THIS CHAPTER
• UNHOOK YOUR MIND FROM WORRRY
• KNOW YOUR CAPABILITIES • YOUR CHECKLIST FOR MINDFUL RESILIENCE

I have explained how fear plays a vital role in helping us to save ourselves from danger. Whether through the response of fight, flight, or freeze, we are equipped with an incredible system for surviving genuine threats to our existence. We instinctively react and, if our reaction is successful, we survive and the danger goes away. If we're not successful, we die.

Fortunately for us humans, the genuine threats to our life are very few – and most of those come from other humans. So our chances of fear ever leading to something life-threatening are extremely slim.

But when the threat is imagined, neither happens. We don't perish but neither does the danger go away. Instead, we are left to live with it, forever battling in our minds trying to fight it, avoid it, or think it through. The heightened state of anxiety that was designed to be used in short bursts to help us survive becomes permanent.

Imaginary dangers are mostly created by our own narrative. Fear that a friend will be annoyed with us, fear that the boss doesn't value us, fear that we won't have time for family and friends, fear of money running out... these typical fears are scenarios conjured up in our own minds.

When we allow our thoughts to override genuine experience, our minds wander into anxiety. We create worst-case scenarios, which then make us anxious, which in turn reduces our resilience to fear and leaves us more anxious still.

We become entangled in a crippling cycle of stress, all because of

A FEAR OF THINGS THAT MIGHT HAPPEN

Imagine lying on your deathbed, looking back on a life of anxiety and realizing that all those things you spent your time worrying about have not happened. You haven't run out of money; you haven't lost your family and friends; your house is still intact; the car is still running... It's comforting to know that all is well before you die, but isn't it a pity – if not a terrible waste – to wait until the end before you appreciate how good life is?!

This is the likely scenario for anyone who spends their time worrying about things that might happen. Because most of the things that we imagine could happen never do.

Why? Because we make sure they don't.

"Ah," you might say, "but that's because we worry about them. If we didn't we wouldn't see them coming and then the worst *would* happen."

Not so.

Seeing problems coming is one thing; worrying about them is another altogether.

Recognizing that there's a possibility of rain before going out for a long walk is a good thing. It enables you to take the necessary precautions, such as sorting out an umbrella, a raincoat, gum-boots perhaps. But once you've taken the precautions, there is no need to worry. You've prevented the possible threat – in this case the threat of getting soaked through – from happening, and so you can enjoy your walk free from anxiety.

Had you not taken precautions before going out, you would have good reason to worry as those dark clouds gather overhead.

If there is something practical you can do to mitigate the likelihood of something bad happening, do it and stop worrying about it. If there's not, then what good is worrying going to do you anyway?

UNHOOK YOUR MIND FROM WORRY

The trouble is the freeze response *does* prevent you from taking action. It can hold you in the grip of paralysis and you end up grappling with the problem endlessly in your mind. The simple precautions that would render the threat non-existent feel beyond you and you get stuck. The fears build up and multiply. The feeling of fear itself becomes a source of anxiety.

Somehow you have to free your mind from the grip of fear. In the counting the breath exercise in Chapter Seven, I suggested you imagine your thoughts as boats going by on a river. Every so often a boat snags you and drags you into the water, making you gasp for breath as you're towed along.

You have to unhook yourself, get back on the riverbank, and observe the boats going by at a safe distance.

The practice of mindfulness enables you to observe your thoughts and worries without getting snagged by them. It is not about conquering fear, but about being aware of your fears and seeing them in their true light, from a detached viewpoint, rather than through the spray and panic as you're dragged along by them.

FIFTH INSTRUCTION: WHENEVER YOU FEEL FEAR, QUESTION IT

Awareness is never more necessary than when you feel threatened. The initial moment when you freeze before instinctively deciding how to respond to fear is when you size up the threat. How big is it? What could it do to me? How can I escape it?

These are valid questions when confronted with danger and they are the questions we run over and over in our minds when the freeze response becomes permanent. But there is one essential question that you can also ask whenever you feel fear:

IS IT REAL?

Because we are conditioned to look for a solution to any problem, we often overlook this obvious question. Instead, we assume that all the threats we perceive are real and proceed to panic, endlessly looking for solutions in our mind.

But when the danger is just not real, there is no solution to be found.

Sometimes, however, you can be afraid of fear itself and it can seem very challenging to look at your fear head on and ask whether it's real or just something you've made up in your imagination. You can free yourself from this grip by accepting that fear is a vital function of your mind and body and, rather than perceive it as a threat that you need to get rid of, accept it as a positive – a function of the incredible machine. That way you will calm your initial response to fear and you will be able to observe more clearly.

YOU WILL BE THE ONE IN CONTROL

The alternative is to bury your head in the sand, or close your eyes and pray, whichever choice of words you prefer. This is a typical freeze response and it is a complete relinquishing of control. When you close your eyes to fear you leave everything to chance. All you can do is hope the danger leaves you alone, but how will you ever know? At what point do you open your eyes?

The answer is never, because until you open your eyes you never know whether or not the danger has passed.

Keep your fears in clear sight and you will see them for what they are. The strange noise at night that turns out to be a water pipe; the shadow that turns out to be a cat; the snapping twig that turns out to be a bird; the phone call that turns out to be good news.

KNOW YOUR CAPABILITIES

As we grow up, we're not taught how to recognize and cope with fear. We're just told "be brave" or "don't worry". It's common for people to endure the symptoms of fear without realizing that it is fear that's causing them. They just feel uncomfortable and uptight without understanding why.

Recognizing how your body responds to fear is a key step in learning how to accept it as a positive not a negative force. Through mindfulness exercises like the body scan, you develop a much closer connection with your sensory system and how it responds to different experiences and emotions. This in turn makes you aware of just how incredible your body is at dealing with threats.

In this way, mindfulness makes you more resilient both physically and mentally. It makes you more confident and better at thinking clearly and rationally, which reduces your susceptibility to fear and increases your power to deal with any sort of threat.

Mindfulness does not remove fear from your life altogether. That isn't the point.

It enables you to accept fear, and the vital role it plays, without getting dragged along by it.

In fact, as you develop the ability to detach from your own fear and observe it, you will begin to be amused by your reactions. Fear is funny. Who, at some point in their life, hasn't had a laugh at someone else's expense by making them jump? You burst a balloon behind their back; leap out at them and surprise them; turn the lights out and make ghostly noises... then you laugh uproariously at the look on their face. We like to play with fear.

We even like to frighten ourselves, whether it's by watching thrillers and horror movies, participating in extreme sports, or going on hair-raising amusement park rides. Notice the name:

"amusement" parks. We put ourselves through fear in the name of amusement.

So it's just a small step to see the humour in your own fear. Again, you have a choice: allow your reaction to fear to become its own source of anxiety, or step back and allow yourself to smile at it.

SIXTH INSTRUCTION:
DON'T TRY TO PROTECT YOURSELF FROM FEAR

YOUR CHECKLIST FOR MINDFUL RESILIENCE

1. Breathe

Taking deep, steady breaths slows your heart rate and activates the body's transition from "flight or flight" back to its calm state, known as "rest and digest". When we're gripped with fear, we can forget to breathe. You literally hold your breath. So be aware of your breathing when you feel anxious and try to maintain a steady, deep breathing as in the counting the breath exercise. Make the "out" breath longer than the "in", i.e. breathe in for a count of 2, breath out for a count of 3 – this is wonderful to relieve fear, anxiety, and stress.

2. Keep things in perspective

First ask yourself if your fear is real. If it is, how serious is it really? Is it a matter of life or death? Are there more important things? Unhook yourself and observe your anxious thoughts rather than getting dragged along by them. That will enable you to see them for what they are.

3. Do something if you can

If something is frightening you, ask yourself what you can do to mitigate the threat. For example, if you're nervous about having to make a speech, you can practise the speech over and over until you know it by heart. That will have the double benefit of removing the fear of forgetting your lines and giving you the best chance of delivering the speech well.

Doing is better than thinking when it comes to stress relief. So if there's something you can do to mitigate your fear, do it. If there's not, then what's the point in worrying?

4. Think positive

As with the steady breathing, you can instigate physical changes by controlling your own behaviour. The mind is malleable. Just as all the brainwashing shapes your brain to think one way, you can shape it to think differently by choosing your own positive thoughts.

The fourth instruction was to pay attention to your positive experiences as they occur. It's important that the positives in your life don't go by unnoticed. By noticing them and reinforcing them with regular reminders, you will reshape the neural pathways in your brain, which in turn will instil a more positive mindset.

5. Laugh

Don't take your fear too seriously. Keep sight of the humour in fearful reactions and allow yourself to laugh at your own reactions to fear.

There is nothing mystical about any of this. It doesn't require meditation, although the techniques learned in meditation can help. It's simply a matter of being aware of what's going on in your mind, not hiding from it, or feeling that you have to conquer it, but observing it with gentleness and keeping it in perspective.

SUMMARY

- **FIFTH INSTRUCTION: WHENEVER YOU FEEL FEAR, QUESTION IT (IS IT REAL?)**

- **Connecting more closely with your physical responses increases confidence**

- **Controlled breathing helps to return your body to "rest and digest"**

- **If you can do something to mitigate a threat, do it. If not, why worry?**

- **Change your mindset with positive thinking**

- **Remember to see the funny side of fear**

- **SIXTH INSTRUCTION: DON'T TRY TO PROTECT YOURSELF FROM FEAR**

CHAPTER 11
BURNING QUESTIONS

IN THIS CHAPTER
• DOES MINDFULNESS MEAN SUPPRESSING MY EMOTIONS?
• SURELY MEDITATING *IS* THINKING? • DO I HAVE TO LEAD A PURE LIFE?
• WHO WILL TACKLE WITH MY ANXIETIES IF I DON'T?
• IF I AM NOT MY THOUGHTS, WHO AM I?
• MY EUREKA MOMENT

I have looked at a lot of aspects of the human body and mind and how they work together and separately. I have examined the way we get stuck in thought and how our attempts to think away difficulties and negative feelings leads to a downward spiral as we pile pressure and frustration on top of our anxieties.

There has been a lot to take in and inevitably questions arise. For most people, the principles of mindfulness involve a whole new way of using your mind. Perhaps you feel that statement alone makes mindfulness sound like something superhuman or mystical, an alien phenomenon that's a bit intimidating.

Rest assured, there is nothing intimidating about practising mindfulness. On the contrary, life is full of intimidating circumstances, which can become overwhelming, leaving us in a tangle of stress and mixed-up emotions. Mindfulness is a method for releasing yourself from that tangle and learning to absorb the impact of life's more intimidating moments.

It requires no special powers. In fact, it unlocks powers you already hold, powers that lie dormant for most of us when we rely on conscious thought as our overriding power.

DOES MINDFULNESS MEAN SUPPRESSING MY EMOTIONS?

I have talked about the need to detach ourselves from our thoughts and learn to observe them in a gentle, non-judgmental way. To some people, this sounds like the sort of instruction a Buddhist master issues to his disciple and the assumption is that it requires you to suppress your emotions so as not to be a slave to them.

Happiness is an emotion and it is formed by a combination of other emotions: love, hope, satisfaction, excitement, pride, gratitude, amusement... If you're feeling any of these positive emotions at any given time, you would probably describe yourself as happy. On the flip side are negative emotions, such as anger, vengeance, envy, malice, hate, and regret. These are all human emotions too and it is generally agreed that both positive and negative emotions play a part in living life "from the heart".

To err is human, as the saying goes, and we tend to regard emotional people as more appealing than those who are ice cool. We like people who show their feelings, especially entertainers, even though they can be high-maintenance. We are drawn to the excitement of passion, which can be both positive and negative.

So the idea of controlling your emotions can be off-putting. You don't want to become unfeeling, cold, and dispassionate.

The good news is in fact, you're learning to do the opposite, to free your feelings, both positive and negative, so that they are neither. With mindfulness, you're not suppressing anything. In fact, you're learning to do the opposite, to free your feelings, both positive and negative, so that they are neither suppressed nor exaggerated.

We suppress emotions when we try to think bad feelings away. When you respond to fear by burying your head in the sand, you are suppressing the negative emotions but not dealing with them, with the result that they fester and multiply.

When we feel overwhelmed by anxious thoughts we shut down the thoughts and emotions that we can't deal with. We anaesthetize ourselves to unpleasant feelings, and so we become less receptive to all our sensory experiences, including the pleasant ones.

We stop noticing the good things in life. We become cynical and unappreciative of the incredible things that are going on around us all the time: buds bursting, insects going about their work, the sunrise, the smell of rain on the pavement, bright sunlight on fresh grass, silence, stillness... We ignore the joyous feelings being picked up by our senses and kid ourselves that there are more sophisticated pleasures to be had.

Having suppressed our ability to appreciate natural pleasures, we seek happiness from artificial "pleasures", including smoking, drinking, gambling, eating junk, buying junk, watching junk. These are not genuine pleasures; they offer nothing more than the illusion of pleasure brought about by brainwashing.

As you become hooked on these false pleasures, their appeal quickly diminishes until you can no longer kid yourself that you're doing it for pleasure and that you're nothing more than a slave, a pathetic addict. The thing you turned to for happiness has made you miserable.

Mindfulness develops greater awareness of your emotions, both positive and negative. It is not an exercise in eradicating emotions but in recognizing them for what they are, putting them in perspective, and allowing them to be, without layering unnecessary discomfort on top of them.

When you try to cling on to good feelings and hide away from bad ones, you add a layer of anxiety to all your emotions, both good and bad. Thus negative emotions become disproportionately painful and positive ones become tainted.

If you can free your mind from this desire to control your emotions and learn to accept them as they are, you will avoid those unnecessary layers of negative emotion. You will also become free to feel the connection between your emotions and your senses, which will enable you to feel genuine happiness.

SURELY MEDITATION *IS* THINKING?

It's a common misconception that meditating is a method for thinking through your problems. In many ways it's the opposite – a method for letting go of your problems, and removing yourself from the constant buzz of distracting thoughts flying around your mind.

Actually, sometimes "letting go" involves learning to accept a situation. For example, if you have an ageing parent that needs care, that is a problem that will continue to exist for an indefinite period. Accepting the situation and doing what we can to manage it practically is key. The situation remains the same, and at times even gets worse. However, our awareness of it, accepting that we cannot fix it, rather than letting that bother us, steers us towards calm rather than constant turmoil.

In mindfulness meditation, you learn that not everything that happens in the mind is thinking. Awareness is observing, and being present with your thoughts and feelings without judgment or recrimination. The fact that you can be aware of your thoughts shows that thoughts are only part of what is going on in your mind.

As with the question of suppressing emotions, mindfulness is not about stopping yourself from thinking, but being able to observe your thoughts and the effect they have on you from a detached, non-judgmental perspective. In doing so, you become more adept at not letting your thoughts run away with you, but keeping them in step with real experience.

The ability to think is one of the most incredible of all the functions of the human machine. It has enabled us to evolve beyond all other creatures on the planet. By learning from experience and visualizing possible outcomes we have made ourselves almost impregnable to danger from other creatures. Our ability to devise solutions, make judgments, put things in order, calculate, and communicate has enabled incredible inventions, buildings, cures, and entertainments.

The downside is that this mental capacity can become obsessed with doing. We see achievement as our only measure of success and view every problem in life as a threat to our need to achieve. Pressure and anxiety are the result.

Fortunately, there is another side to our mental capacity – a side that derives contentment from being. This is the part of the brain that we access through mindfulness. It is the part that is in touch with our sensory experience and it is able to accept the ebb and flow of life's fortunes with interest rather than judgment.

Mindfulness is not dependent on meditation. As shown by Ellen Langer's Counterclockwise Experiment, there are other ways to change a person's mindset to have a positive effect on their physical and mental health. But the practice of meditation does help to develop the ability to let go of your thoughts.

In this helter-skelter world, it is all too easy to get carried along by the current and feel that you never have time for contemplation. Making meditation part of your routine helps to ensure that you spend part of each day in deeper observation and awareness. In this relaxed, serene situation, it is easier to achieve a non-judgmental, accepting mindset, allowing everything, both good and bad, to exist without fighting to cling on to it or eliminate it.

Regard the mindfulness exercises as individual exercises in achieving awareness, rather than a general activity called "meditation". If, as a result of doing the exercises, you achieve the relaxed, serene, enlightened state that we call meditation, then that's a sign that you are following the instructions correctly.

DO I HAVE TO LEAD A PURE LIFE?

Once again, the association of mindfulness with ascetic Buddhist monks creates unhelpful preconceptions. Let us state quite clearly, here and now, that you are not required to sacrifice all that you hold dear and go and live in a cave!

Indeed, there is no need to impose any restrictions on yourself whatsoever. Feeling deprived is not conducive to happiness. Deprivation heightens desire. This is the problem smokers and other addicts encounter when they try to quit with the willpower method. They force themselves to go without their little crutch and feel deprived as a result. This increases their desire for it and reinforces the illusion of pleasure. Rather than quitting becoming easier with time, it becomes harder and harder until they can resist no longer.

That's why people who try to quit with the willpower method nearly always fall back into the trap. And when they do they fall in deeper than before because their failure reinforces the belief that it's almost impossible to quit and that they can't live without their little crutch. The huge relief they feel when they capitulate is misinterpreted as pleasure.

I realized that quitting was only hard if you retained the desire to smoke. The desire is formed by brainwashing. By helping smokers to be more aware of the real experience of smoking and to observe their reasons for smoking and the truth behind those reasons, Easyway removes the desire *before* you smoke your final cigarette.

As you become better connected with your senses through mindfulness, you will start to see that the pleasure or crutch you think you derive from those artificial stimulants is illusory and your desire for smoking, drinking, junk food, etc., will go. You will also see through the myths that make it hard to quit – myths such as "smoking relaxes you" and "drinking makes you more sociable".

If you're someone who smokes or does anything that you

perceive as a pleasure or crutch, even though you know it's bad for you, try taking a mindful approach to it from now on. Go back to the mindful berry-eating exercise in Chapter One and apply the same approach to your next cigarette, drink, or whatever. Really pay attention to how you react at each stage of the process: how it feels in your hand, how your heart beats, how it really tastes, smells, and feels in your mouth. Focus on the sensory experience throughout and ask yourself if this is really as good in the reality of the present as it seems in your recollection.

The artificial stimulants you turn to for relief and pleasure also have an impact on you physically. Physical condition has a direct effect on mental wellbeing. As you feel physically stronger and cleaner, your mental happiness will improve. This in turn will have a positive effect on your physical wellbeing and the cycle will turn from a downward spiral of misery to a virtuous circle of happiness.

WHO WILL TACKLE MY ANXIETIES IF I DON'T?

This question presupposes that the way to remove anxieties is to tackle them. That is like saying the way to untangle a bundle of string is to pull hard on the ends. All you achieve with that approach is tighter knots and a more baffling tangle. With mindfulness, you take a gentle, observant approach that allows the tangles to fall out.

Detaching from your thoughts does not mean dismissing them. And letting go does not mean not bothering. The fact is, without mindfulness, we don't bother a lot of the time. We push feelings and problems aside, bury our head in the sand, and deny reality. Does this make the anxieties go away? Not at all.

The answer to this question is quite straightforward: mindfulness *is* the way for *you* to deal with your anxieties. By developing a method for observing them calmly and keeping them in perspective, you make it easier for you to live with your own anxieties without being dragged under by them. You don't need anyone else, or anything else, to help you cope.

IF I AM NOT MY THOUGHTS, WHO AM I?

Because we set so much store by our thoughts, we tend to base our perception of who we are on the thoughts we have. In this way we become susceptible to developing a negative perception of "me". "I'm a smoker", for example, rather than "I'm a person who smokes". This fixed self-image makes it harder to change our behaviour. If you're a person who smokes, it's easy to see yourself becoming a person who does not smoke. But if you're a smoker, what would you be without smoking?

The fear of life after smoking is a big factor in smokers failing to quit. If you believe that a part of you will be missing without cigarettes, then the fear of quitting can outweigh the fear of continuing to smoke.

The fact is there is much more to us than our thoughts. The physical functions that keep us alive – e.g. breathing, circulation, digestion – happen without conscious thought. The same is true of our instinctive reactions, and even many of the decisions we make happen before we are conscious of them. Have you ever been driving and realized that you can't remember anything from the last couple of miles? You've succeeded in driving without incident, observing the rules of the road, and negotiating the twists and turns of the highway, but you don't remember being conscious of any of it because your thoughts were elsewhere.

The evidence is clear:

THERE MUST BE MUCH MORE TO WHO YOU ARE THAN YOUR THOUGHTS

When you accept this you begin to access a new level of mental freedom. You recognize that you are not responsible for everything that happens in your life and you can give yourself a break from having to sort it all out. You become more accepting of the experiences in your life, both positive and negative, and release yourself from the struggle between what *is* and what you *want to be*.

You stop seeing life as a collection of fixed situations that you need to either cling to or avoid, and recognize that everything is in a constant state of change. Instead of digging your heels in and trying to turn back the tide, you learn to ride the waves, leading to a lighter, more positive state of mind.

MY EUREKA MOMENT

Before I discovered the cure for smoking, I was like so many other smokers: desperate to quit but incapable of doing so because, I thought, of a flaw in my own personality. No matter how hard I tried, I simply couldn't stay off the cigarettes. I felt responsible and, therefore, my failure made me feel weak and helpless.

This compounded my misery, which drove me deeper into the arms of nicotine addiction.

The trigger that changed my mindset was the moment when I thought about it being addiction for the first time. It was a lightbulb moment. The effect was instantaneous. A chance remark changed my whole way of thinking, from assuming I was the one in control and, therefore, the one responsible for my failure to quit, to recognizing that I was not in control and, therefore, could not be held responsible for my failure. It also made me realize that I didn't smoke because I wanted to or chose to but because I was in a trap called addiction. Choice wasn't involved.

This realization had a powerful liberating effect. I was able to see that all I had to do to free myself from the trap was to stop smoking. The rest would be easy. By letting go of responsibility, I was able to take control.

As a human being you are an incredible amalgamation of thoughts, subconscious, automatic functions, sensory perceptions, and conditioned behaviours. It's important that you recognize this and accept it.

You are so much more than your thoughts, so don't be frustrated or disappointed that you can't always think your way past problems.

BE AWARE AND ACCEPT THE THINGS YOU CAN'T CONTROL

*THIS WILL FREE YOUR MIND TO BETTER CONTROL
THE THINGS YOU CAN*

SUMMARY

- Mindfulness develops a greater awareness of emotions, good and bad

- Try to find time for quiet contemplation each day

- Aim to pursue genuine pleasures rather than false ones. Your mind and body will benefit

- A gentle approach is the best way to untangle anxieties

- Remember you are much more than your thoughts

- Accept the things you can't control

- Letting go of the struggle helps you gain control

IN THIS CHAPTER
• "I AM AN ADDICT" • EBB AND FLOW
• NOTHING IS FIXED • SEEING THROUGH ILLUSIONS
• NO LONGER OVERWHELMED IN THOUGHT

When our thoughts wander to the subject of ourselves, they tend to construct negative identities.

• I'M TOO FAT

• I'M TOO THIN

• I'M TOO OLD

• I'M POOR

• I'M ILL

• I'M UNFIT

• I'M LAZY

• I'M WEAK-WILLED

• I'M UNLUCKY

The tendency towards self-criticism takes place against a backdrop of yearning for happiness, which is doomed to remain unfulfilled by the very fact that we are forever striving for it, trying to pounce on good experiences, and hide from bad ones. In short, we blame ourselves for our inability to find the happiness we crave.

It's not hard to find shortcomings in ourselves. Nobody is perfect. But things that we're happy to forgive in others we refuse to let go in ourselves. We take ownership of our perceived shortcomings and make them our identity.

This constant self-analysis takes place without really looking, listening, and seeing the truth, and so it is not a sensory perception of who we really are. It's a fixed idea of the person we wish we weren't.

When we focus on the aspects of ourselves that we don't like, it makes us miserable. Yet the aspects we most commonly dislike about ourselves are caused by pursuing activities that we mistakenly believe will alleviate that misery: eating, drinking, smoking... All these so-called "pursuits of pleasure" make us unfit, overweight, sluggish, lethargic, ill, pallid, and poor.

So we become trapped in a vicious circle. The more you seek relief from misery in things like eating, drinking, and smoking, the more your physical condition deteriorates and the more miserable you become. But when you get stuck with a fixed perception of yourself, your behaviour conforms to that identity.

I'M FAT – THEREFORE, I WILL EAT JUNK

**I'M UNFIT – THEREFORE, I WON'T WALK,
I'LL TAKE THE CAR**

**I'M WEAK-WILLED –
THEREFORE, THERE'S NO POINT IN TRYING**

This is particularly well demonstrated by…

THE MYTH OF THE ADDICTIVE PERSONALITY

Many people with addictions believe that there's something in their genetic make-up that makes them more susceptible than most to getting hooked and makes it harder for them to escape. They form their own fixed identity.

"I AM AN ADDICT"

Sadly, their misconception is supported by a number of so-called "experts", who support the theory of the addictive personality. The term is bandied about so often that it's easy to be fooled into believing that it's an established condition.

IT IS NOT!

The addictive personality is a theory put forward to try and explain the incidence of repeated failures to quit and multiple addictions in the same people, e.g. drinkers who are also smokers or gamblers, or heroin addicts who smoke and are heavily in debt.

All these addictions are caused by the same thing but it's not the personality: it's the misguided belief that the thing you are addicted to gives you a genuine pleasure or crutch. Remember,

THE MISERY OF ADDICTION IS NOT RELIEVED BY THE THING YOU ARE ADDICTED TO; IT'S CAUSED BY IT

The fear of success drives people with addictions to seek reasons to avoid even trying to quit. The addictive personality theory gives them the perfect excuse. If you think you have an addictive personality, you will regard quitting as an impossible task. "How can I override my own genetic make-up?"

This illusion can also be reinforced by your failed attempts to quit by using willpower.

It is further confirmed by people who have quit by using the willpower method and are feeling deprived because they still believe they're making a sacrifice. After all, if they have abstained for years and are still craving their little crutch, surely there must be some flaw in their genetic make-up that keeps drawing them back?

But there is another explanation, and one that has been proven by Easyway time and time again.

THE FEAR OF SUCCESS IS BASED ON AN ILLUSION

– the illusion that you are making a genuine sacrifice.

People who whinge about having quit are constantly tormented because they still believe that they are depriving themselves. Don't be fooled by these illusions. You are not "giving up" anything when you quit. All you are doing is making marvellous gains. Pleading that you can't quit because you have an addictive personality is just a feeble excuse.

Escape from addiction is easy, provided you keep an open mind and follow the right method. If you cling to the excuse that you have an addictive personality, it means that your mind is not open and you risk sentencing yourself to remain trapped for the rest of your life.

So why do some people fall deeper into the trap than others? Why can one person have the occasional drink, while another ends up reaching for the booze first thing in the morning? Doesn't that suggest that one has an addictive personality and the other doesn't?

It does point to a difference between them, yes, but there are numerous differences between people, which can explain why one's behaviour differs from another's in this context, and none of them has anything to do with having an addictive personality.

For most people, the first experience of drinking is revolting. For some, that's enough to put them off ever drinking again. Others see it as a challenge that must be surmounted if they are to earn respect, and make a point of drinking as much as they can. Others can't afford to drink more than a small amount each week. In addition to that, our behaviour is closely linked to the influences we are subjected to as we grow up: different parents, teachers, friends, things we read, watch and listen to, places we go, people we meet, etc.

All these factors will have a bearing on how quickly we descend into the trap. The celebrities that we hear about who seem to fall so rapidly into alcoholism or drug addiction usually have millions to pour down the drain, and the time and opportunity to do so.

Birds of a feather flock together, as the old saying goes, and that is certainly true of people with addictions. Smokers seek the company of other smokers. Drinkers prefer to drink with other drinkers. People who overeat feel more comfortable in the company of other overeaters. They share similar character traits: an unstable temperament, a tendency towards excess, a high susceptibility to stress, evasiveness, anxiety, insecurity.

The addictive personality theory has jumped on this as evidence that there is a "type" that tends to fall into the trap. The reality is that all these shared traits are the *result* of addiction and the reason they like to flock together is because they don't feel so stupid among other addicts. They're all in the same boat.

The good news is that, once you're free from the addiction, you also get free from the harmful effects it has on your character.

Advocates of the addictive personality theory like to draw on statistics, but the statistics actually make the theory look ridiculous. If there were a gene that predisposed people to become addicts, you would expect the percentage of addicts in the world to have remained fairly constant throughout history, would you not? Yet this is not the case.

Take smoking: in the 1940s more than 80 per cent of the adult male population in the UK was hooked on nicotine; today it's less than 20 per cent. A similar trend is evident throughout most of Western Europe and North America. So are we to conclude that the proportion of people with addictive personalities has fallen by a whopping 60 per cent in just over half a century?

At the same time, the number of smokers in Asia has soared. Could a genetic anomaly really rise and fall so rapidly, and even transfer itself wholesale from one continent to another?

Of course not.

People with addictions take a big step closer to freedom when they realize that they didn't become addicted because they have an addictive personality. If you think you have an addictive personality, it's simply because you got addicted. You got addicted because you took an addictive drug.

This is the trick that addiction plays on you. It makes you feel that you're dependent on your little crutch and that there's some weakness in your character or genetic make-up. It distorts your perceptions and thereby maintains its grip on you.

The addictive personality theory encourages the belief that escape is out of your hands and that you are condemned to a life of slavery. You forget that you didn't feel any need or desire for your little crutch until you started taking it. It was the act of taking it that created the addiction, not the other way around.

Just keep an open mind and keep following all the instructions.

SEVENTH INSTRUCTION:
LET GO OF ANY FIXED IDENTITY

EBB AND FLOW

Keeping hold of fixed ideas of yourself is not only unhelpful in establishing a positive mindset, it is also illogical. How can you have a fixed identity when the person you are is constantly changing?

Was the childhood "you" the same as "you" today? Did you have the same beliefs, fears, hopes, relationships, and knowledge? Were you stressed, depressed, or addicted? These problems are rare in childhood. They are normally a consequence of growing up, taking on responsibilities, becoming overwhelmed, not knowing how to cope, reaching for relief, failing to find any calmness, or quiet.

But these problems are not fixed in adulthood. They come and go all the time, changing from day to day, from moment to moment. When you practise the body scan, be aware of the changes being picked up by your senses from one moment to the next. Just as your body is constantly changing, cells dying, and new ones being produced, your mind and personality changes too. The mind adapts to experience and new information. Repeated experiences form new patterns of behaviour. But these patterns can be undone again.

NOTHING IS FIXED

So the idea that you can or can't do something because of your personality is utterly flawed. The more we learn about the brain, the more it becomes evident that it is malleable, and we can "rewire" it to change those patterns of behaviour for the better. But we know that anyway. Isn't that what education is all about: changing our mental state from one of ignorance to one of knowledge?

Addiction changes your mindset too. Anyone who smokes or drinks will remember that first-ever taste of a cigarette or alcoholic drink: how vile it was; how it made them choke; how their body instinctively tried to expel the poison. How could something so foul become your best friend? But for people with nicotine and alcohol addiction it does. It also becomes their worst enemy.

If the mind can be "rewired" to believe that a poison does

you good, it can be "rewired" to undo that misconception too. That is how Easyway works. And it has proven to be the most successful way to cure addiction.

SEEING THROUGH ILLUSIONS

Do you regard yourself as an open-minded person? The third instruction was to keep an open mind and hopefully you've been following it, but it's a fact that we go through life with our minds largely made up by other people. For example, when you see the sun rise in the morning, you interpret it as a ball of fiery gases burning millions of miles away, which has the appearance of rising in the sky because the Earth is spinning. How do you know that's the case? Because you've been presented with some very convincing arguments by people with expertise in that field, none of whom have yet contradicted the theory, and the explanation tallies with what you see.

Not so long ago, people firmly believed that the sun was actually God driving a fiery chariot across the sky. That was the explanation put forward by the learned men of the time and it tallied with what people saw. So bear in mind:

WHAT WE BELIEVE IS RARELY BASED ON THE EVIDENCE OF OUR OWN INVESTIGATIONS

WHAT WE ARE TOLD BY SO-CALLED EXPERTS IS OFTEN UNTRUE

We have demonstrated how quickly and easily the mind can be "rewired" with the table illusion in Chapter Four.

The illusion demonstrates three key aspects of the human mind. Firstly, how easily it can be tricked into believing something that is false. Secondly, how easily your mindset changes when you are given more convincing evidence – in this case measuring the tables "rewires" your mind to see them both as identical.

And thirdly, once your mind has seen through the illusion and knows the truth,

IT CANNOT BE FOOLED AGAIN

Many of the causes of unhappiness are brought about by being brainwashed with false beliefs, e.g.:

THE BELIEF THAT SMOKING IS COOL AND RELAXES YOU

THE BELIEF THAT ALCOHOL MAKES YOU MORE GROWN-UP AND SOCIABLE

THE BELIEF THAT SUGARY FOODS ARE THE TASTIEST

THE BELIEF THAT YOU CHOOSE ALL THESE THINGS OF YOUR OWN FREE WILL.

The question is, when we realize that these things are actually making us unhappy, why don't we change our mindset and stop choosing them? There are two main reasons:

1.   The fear of success

2.   We don't realize we have a choice.

Remember, the fear of success is based on illusions. Open your mind to what your senses are telling you – that these little crutches do nothing for you whatsoever – and to the possibility that life without them will be better and you will not feel deprived at all.

When you are made aware that you do have a choice to see things differently, the picture beings to change. Open your mind, use your own senses to see things as they really are, and you will find your mind relaxing, letting go of fixed ideas, and seeing the truth more clearly.

NO LONGER OVERWHELMED IN THOUGHT

Mindfulness teaches you to notice your own thinking. It lifts you out of your own thoughts to a position of gentle observation, so you are no longer in the box of flies, no longer overwhelmed.

Thoughts will still happen, good and bad, but you learn to see them as one function of your mind, rather than a definition of who you are.

Thinking is the great trump card of the human race, but it comes with baggage, fixed ideas of hope, fear, desire, regret, etc. All these emotions add stress to the thoughts, an unnecessary weight that is hard to carry and adds to the pressure. When you let go of your thoughts, you put down that baggage and observe the thought alone.

We use the expression "lighten up". When you put down the baggage that comes with your thoughts, that's exactly what you feel, a wonderful lightness of mind, which leads to a more positive mindset. This makes you stronger and better able to handle any unpleasant thoughts and sensations that arise. When you put down the baggage, you remove the layer of panic that accompanies unpleasant thoughts and feelings, thus reducing their impact.

You become more resilient in the face of pain and bad news.

The key for someone who thinks they have an addictive personality is to change from regarding themselves as "an addict" to "someone with an addiction". It may seem like a subtle difference but the effect can be life-changing. An addict is stuck. Someone with an addiction can become someone without an addiction.

This isn't just a principle for addiction; it applies to any negative identity that you might attach to yourself. As you become more practised at mindfulness and your awareness of real experience increases, so you start to release yourself from mindlessly following fixed ideas and practices. Like untangling a ball of string, you can gently free yourself from negativity.

SUMMARY

- **Your behaviour conforms to fixed ideas of "self"**
- **There is no such thing as an addictive personality**
- **SEVENTH INSTRUCTION: LET GO OF ANY FIXED IDENTITY**
- **The person you are is constantly changing**
- **Once you've seen through an illusion, you cannot be fooled by it again**
- **Let go of your thoughts and put down the baggage**

CHAPTER 13
WILLPOWER

IN THIS CHAPTER
• Herding frogs • The power of letting go • Willpower and addiction
• How weak-willed are you? • Facing your demons gently

Do you find that every time you try to change a fundamental aspect of your life, such as your diet, it feels incredibly hard and you end up giving in? And is your conclusion always the same?

"I DON'T HAVE THE WILLPOWER"

This is typical of a fixed identity creating a negative mindset. As soon as you tell yourself you don't have the willpower, you ensure that you will fail. You see yourself as a weak-willed person and subconsciously strive to fulfil that identity. Failure becomes your comfort zone and while you might put yourself through the mental struggle you think is required to succeed, you take actions that you know subconsciously will prove your belief that you *don't* have what it takes. Get it clear in your mind:

EVERYBODY HAS WHAT IT TAKES

From birth, we are given the tools to be healthy and happy. It's brainwashing that influences us to lead unhealthy, stressful, anxious lives. And part of the brainwashing is the false belief that any achievement requires a certain degree of suffering.

Whether it's quitting smoking, avoiding junk food, getting fit, or learning a new skill, we assume that there will be some hardship involved, either physical or mental, or both. We define willpower as the mental strength to push on through the pain.

HERDING FROGS

This obsession with willpower connects to our tendency to seek happiness by trying to cling on to pleasant experiences and fight off unpleasant ones.

Do you ever ask yourself:

WHY DOES EVERYTHING HAVE TO BE A STRUGGLE?

We are taught from a young age that the only way to achieve success is through determination and effort. This may be a valid assertion when it comes to building a career or a house, but it is not a blanket rule for all aspects of life.

Do you need determination to build a relationship with someone you love? Isn't it the easiest, most natural thing in the world?

Do you require effort <u>not</u> to open a bottle of wine? Compared to the effort that goes into drinking, not drinking is a walk in the park. Yet when you're hooked on alcohol, you regard <u>not</u> drinking as the worst ordeal.

We equate willpower with control.

"GET A GRIP"

"KNUCKLE DOWN"

"PUT YOUR MIND TO IT"

Yet we all know that we cannot control every aspect of our lives in this way. As soon as we think we've gained control over one problem, another pops up elsewhere. It's like trying to herd frogs.

What if I told you that willpower actually makes it harder for you to take control? It goes against everything we're brought up to believe, yet there is no shortage of evidence that it's true. The more we strive for happiness, the more stressed we become, and thus the more unhappy.

If you have ever lain awake at night tormented by anxieties, you will know how ineffective willpower is for solving problems. You lie there in the dark, craving the mental calm to be able to sleep, but tossing and turning as your head fills with anxious thoughts that you try to control by grappling with them in your mind. The more you wrack your brain for solutions, the more tense and anxious you become.

You're so determined to work out a solution to your problems that you won't let go and allow yourself to get the sleep you so badly need. But you can't do anything about your problems when you're lying in bed at night, so thinking about them and willing them away only adds to the stress. Your ability to see solutions diminishes when you're stressed.

THE POWER OF LETTING GO

The fear is that if we just let things be, nothing will change. But things change all the time, whether we make them or not. The world around you is constantly changing and so are you. The control we try to exert through willpower is more often focused on preventing change. We want certainty, familiarity, predictability, so we try to tie things down. But, like the frogs, it's impossible to make everything in life stand still, so our efforts are thwarted.

A swimmer who is caught in a riptide has two choices: swim with all their might against the tide or relax and see where it takes them. Those who choose the former course are more likely to drown. They quickly become exhausted, swallow too much water, and sink. Those who relax and go with the flow may be taken somewhere they weren't expecting, but they stay afloat and reach calmer water with the energy to swim ashore.

By letting things be, we allow the natural to take its course and our lives to move with the changes. This leaves us more relaxed and energized, and so much better placed to make sound decisions and see them through.

Rather than grapple with your anxieties, you need to let go of them or bring an acceptance to them. Let them be.

You might feel anxious about public speaking. That anxiety might remain, but you no longer have to react to the symptoms. It's okay to be anxious; we are present to it, so it no longer controls our behaviour or performance. If you still find it hard to believe that this can make a difference, that's okay as long as you remember the instructions. All you need to do is follow them and you will discover the truth for yourself.

EIGHTH INSTRUCTION:
LET GO OF YOUR RELIANCE ON WILLPOWER

WILLPOWER AND ADDICTION

With Easyway, I came up with a perfect illustration of the power of letting go. I claimed that I could help smokers quit without the need for willpower and proceeded to prove the point. But I went a step further, stating categorically that people who tried to quit with the willpower method were almost guaranteed to fail.

There is one simple reason why anybody finds it hard to quit smoking, drinking, or any other addiction: they are using the wrong method.

The simplest of tasks becomes difficult if you go about it the wrong way. For example, opening a door. You know how to open a door – you push on the handle and it swings open with the minimum of effort.

But have you ever come across a door with no handle and pushed on the wrong side, where the hinges are? You're met with firm resistance. The door might shift a tiny bit, but it won't swing open. It requires a huge amount of effort and determination. Push on the correct side and the door opens without you even having to think about it.

Most addicts find it difficult to stop because they use the willpower method. It's not their fault. All the received wisdom is that you need willpower to quit. Only Easyway takes the opposite view. People who try to quit with the willpower method endure a constant conflict of will, a mental tug-of-war.

On one side, your rational brain knows you should stop because it's making you ill, affecting your behaviour, costing you a fortune, controlling your life, and causing you misery. On the other side, your addicted brain makes you panic at the thought of being deprived of your little crutch.

With the willpower method, you focus on all the negative outcomes of continuing, and hope you can deny yourself long enough for the desire to eventually go.

With Easyway, you see the positive outcomes of stopping and thus remove the desire to continue altogether.

The fundamental problem with the willpower method is that you remain under the illusion that you're giving up a pleasure or crutch. You believe you're making a sacrifice. But you want to quit so you will yourself into a self-imposed tantrum, like a child being deprived of its toys. The feeling of deprivation makes you miserable, which in turn makes you want to try to cheer yourself up – and the way you always do that is to turn to your little crutch.

EASYWAY REMOVES THE NEED FOR WILLPOWER BY REMOVING THE ILLUSION THAT YOU'RE MAKING A SACRIFICE

Some people do manage to stop themselves drinking, smoking, gambling, etc., through sheer force of will, but they never actually break free of the addiction. They remain vulnerable to it, feeling a sense of loss and deprivation that never goes away. In most cases, the willpower method fails and they end up back in the trap, feeling more helpless and miserable than before.

Encouraging someone to quit through the use of willpower is like telling them to open a door by pushing on the hinges.

When you try to quit by the willpower method, the struggle never ends. As long as you continue to believe that you're giving something up, you will always be running in pain. The stronger your will, the longer you will withstand the agony. But the agony only gets worse because the longer you go on suffering a sense of deprivation, the more powerful your craving becomes.

With Easyway, the elation of getting free occurs as soon as you remove the fear and illusions. That's when you are free of the addiction that has kept you enslaved. There's no suffering involved and you don't need to wait for anything else to happen.

The psychology of the addict is such that a hardline approach will not work. Rather than helping you to quit, it actually encourages you to stay hooked because:

1.   It reinforces the myth that quitting is hard and, therefore, adds to your fear.

2.   It creates a feeling of deprivation, which you will seek to alleviate by turning to your little crutch.

Once you have failed on the willpower method, it's even harder to try again because you will have reinforced the belief that it is impossible to cure your problem. People who have tried the willpower method and failed will tell you they felt an enormous sense of relief when they gave in. It's important to understand that this relief is nothing more than a temporary end to the self-inflicted pain. They don't think, "Great! I've fallen back into the trap." It is not a pleasure. In fact, it is accompanied by feelings of failure and foreboding, guilt, and disappointment.

It is important that you ignore the advice of anyone who claims to have quit by the willpower method. The beautiful truth is there is no sacrifice. You need only to understand that you are not "giving up" anything. You only need willpower if you are caught up in the tug-of-war of fear. Take away the fear and there is nothing to tug against. It's easy.

HOW WEAK-WILLED ARE YOU?

Just as the willpower method is commonly assumed to be the only way to succeed at curing an addiction, those who fail to quit that way and remain in the trap are widely branded as weak-willed. Indeed, they brand themselves as weak-willed. They assume it's they who have failed, not the method.

If you're in a position where you're struggling to change an aspect of your life and think you lack the willpower, ask yourself whether you're weak-willed in other ways.

Smokers who attend my centres often feel that they are weak-willed. But I ask them to remember how they started smoking in the first place, including the effort it took to get past the initial revulsion at their first cigarettes. It's the same with drinkers who seek our help. No matter how low the drug may have dragged them down – making them increasingly stressed and unhappy, threatening to destroy their relationships, their health, their career, their lives – they have still continued to take it.

That sort of persistence is not the behaviour of a weak-willed person. That's leaving aside the extent they'd go to in order to manipulate people and situations to enable them to carry on with the drug.

If you saw someone trying to open a door by pushing on the hinges and you told them they would find it easier if they pushed on the handle, but they ignored you and insisted on pushing on the hinges, you'd call them wilful, not weak-willed.

There are enough high-profile examples to illustrate that addiction is not exclusive to the weak-willed. Presidents, captains of industry, movie stars, singers, sports stars, writers... my stop-smoking and stop-drinking seminars, as well as my seminars that deal with drugs such as heroin and cocaine, are attended by people who have often found tremendous success in life: in business, medicine, music, drama, and professional sport – they represent a wide cross-section of professions and vocations that require incredible dedication, guts, ability, and determination. In other words, they have immense willpower. So why would their willpower fail them in this one area?

In fact, it tends to be the most strong-willed people who find it hardest to quit by using the willpower method. Why? Because when the door fails to open, they won't give up and try to find an easier method; they'll force themselves to keep pushing on the hinges until they can push no more. They blame themselves.

Willpower is a function of the human brain designed for survival, not happiness. If you need to climb a tree to escape a predator, or you need to build a shelter in a storm, willpower could be invaluable. But when you use willpower to tackle imaginary threats that are conjured up in your mind, all you're doing is pushing hard on the wrong side of the door.

FACING YOUR DEMONS GENTLY

With mindfulness, you develop your ability to manage your reaction and response to unpleasant experiences, so you no longer react to them by fighting them off, thinking them through, or denying their existence, but bring your attention to them gently.

You may well find this challenging to begin with, but as you become more practised at it, you will see how your demons become far less daunting when you accept their existence non-judgmentally and, in many cases, they disappear altogether.

Next time you practise the body scan, take notice of any unpleasant sensations. Are you feeling pain anywhere? What about emotional pain? Pinpoint where these pains stem from and what feelings they stir. Is it a sharp pain, a dull ache, a stinging sensation? How is the pain manifested? Pay attention to the reactions these sensations produce. Do you feel like fighting them, thinking them through, or avoiding them? Take interest in your reactions without allowing them to take hold.

Pick on one area where you're detecting unpleasant sensations and home in on it. Use your body scan skills to focus on the area and feel exactly what's going on. Remember, this is a gentle exercise. You're not going in to sort it out. Whatever the sensation is, however the pain manifests itself, accept that it exists and just watch it with interest, like watching a wild animal from a safe distance.

Gradually move in closer, breathing steadily and resisting any impulse to tackle it or turn away from it. Notice the sensation in detail. How does it change from moment to moment? Be aware of any thoughts that arise and let them pass across your mind like boats on a river. Let go.

The practice of turning towards difficulty has been shown to reduce the stress caused by unpleasant experiences. It's when your mind wanders that the negative thoughts pile in and the stress builds up. Being present with your experiences without feeling compelled to tackle them makes them less threatening, even when those experiences are not pleasant.

SUMMARY

- **Everybody has what it takes to succeed**

- **Willpower makes it harder to take control**

- **Things change all the time; go with the flow!**

- **EIGHTH INSTRUCTION: LET GO OF YOUR RELIANCE ON WILLPOWER**

- **The willpower method of curing addiction is doomed to failure**

- **Many strong-willed people have addictions**

- **Being present with difficulty makes it less stressful**

CHAPTER 14
CUTTING OUT THE NOISE

IN THIS CHAPTER
• QUESTIONING INFORMATION AND BELIEFS • A PROBLEM SHARED
• CUTTING OUT THE NOISE IN THE NIGHT • LETTING GO OF THE STRUGGLE
• EXERCISE: MINDFUL LISTENING

So let's recap what we've established so far. I've explained how the mind, when allowed to wander, tends to wander into negativity. Our instinct for survival, coupled with the intellectual capacity to foresee danger, has created a bias towards focusing on the worst-case scenario.

This is a valuable trait when avoiding genuine dangers, but the sort of "dangers" we encounter in modern life are far from life-threatening. In many cases, they don't even exist; we obsess about the possibility that they *could* exist. And as a result we suffer anxieties created by our own imagination.

We've also explained how we get stuck in fixed ways of thinking that become our identity.

"I'M NOT GOOD ENOUGH"

"I DON'T BELONG"

"I'M WEAK-WILLED"

These negative thoughts become our perception of reality, and reach a point where we only feel comfortable when we confirm our own negative beliefs. If you label yourself as weak-willed, anything you might want to achieve is doomed to failure because you subconsciously sabotage your own efforts, so that you can say to yourself, "See, I knew it. I am weak-willed."

Failure becomes a comfort blanket. The idea of success becomes a source of fear because it will take you somewhere unfamiliar. So you become stuck in a tug-of-war: not happy with the way things are but fearful of doing anything different. Damned if you do, damned if you don't. The result is unhappiness.

This negative identity gives you the excuse you need not to try to change. In an extreme case like smoking, the belief that you have an addictive personality gives you the excuse to remain in your comfort zone of failure, living the life of a slave, knowing that you're killing yourself, wasting your money, upsetting your loved ones, but afraid of what life would be like without smoking.

All addicts find themselves in the tug-of-war of fear, afraid of the damage they're doing to themselves and their relationship with those around them, but also terrified of life without their little crutch.

But the tug-of-war doesn't just apply to people with addictions; it's there with everyday anxieties too.

Perhaps you have bills to pay and they're becoming overdue, but you're worried that you'll be left with no money if you pay them all off. So you bury your head in the sand and leave them, hoping that if you ignore them you might be able to pretend they don't exist. Of course, you can't fool yourself in this way. The pressure to pay those outstanding bills is a constant anxiety in your mind, as is the fear of how you'll end up if you do pay them.

So you have a double fear: partly real, partly imagined. Now, what would happen if you dealt with the real fear? If you paid the bills, you would remove the anxiety they're causing while they remain unpaid.

Okay, so you might have no money left afterwards, but you're still better off for two reasons:

1. You've removed the double fear of the unpaid bills and the worry about having no money after you've paid them.

2. You can see the situation as it really is, rather than a situation you've created in your mind.

Chances are your financial situation after you've paid the bills won't be as bad as you had imagined. Remember, when we rely on our imagination in such situations, we tend to imagine the worst-case scenario. Even if you are left with no money, the pressure is off because you've paid all your bills. How good does that feel!

By taking action to address the genuine source of fear, you have removed one major source of anxiety and reduced another. As a result, you feel much less stressed and better able to think clearly about your next move: how to build up your bank balance again.

Thoughts can transfix us like rabbits in the headlights, leaving us stuck in the tug-of-war of fear. When you can see that thoughts are not reality but just one function of your brain, and that nothing is ever fixed but always changing, it becomes easier to free yourself from the tug-of-war of fear, address the genuine threats, and free yourself from the fear of imaginary ones.

Our ability to think is a wonderful attribute. We can project into the future and weigh up the past in a way that leads to incredible invention.

But it also backfires when we allow our imagination to run away with us and invent scenarios that cause stress. If you trust your imagination over your senses, your perception of reality separates you from what is real.

In other words, you lose sight of how things really are; you miss out on the good things that are happening all around you; and you layer unnecessary anxiety on top of the bad things.

Through mindfulness, you learn to change your perspective on thoughts and see them as they really are – one function of your brain – and you develop the ability to observe them without judgment. You learn not to fight off anxious thoughts but to allow them to exist and observe them with interest, thus avoiding the extra layers of anxiety and stress that make any small concern a big one.

Whenever your thoughts begin to wander into negativity, you are aware of their wandering and can gently bring your mind back to the present, to breathing, to observing rather than being caught up in negative thought.

QUESTIONING INFORMATION AND BELIEFS

Much of the stress that we endure is brought on through brainwashing. Our heads are filled with instructions about who we should be, how we should behave, how we should look, what we should eat, what we should have… the list is almost endless.

Rather than making decisions based on what's really happening, your judgment is clouded by all these mixed messages and false information, causing a tension between what you feel and what you think.

The solutions you come up with don't lead to satisfaction because they are designed for a problem that doesn't exist. Again, we can use the example of smoking. It's widely believed that you can make it easier to quit smoking if you replace the cigarette with a less toxic substitute, such as nicotine gum or an e-cigarette. The theory is that you can continue to give yourself doses of the drug while you get out of the habit of smoking, then gradually reduce the dose until you're ready to kick the drug too.

Unfortunately, it doesn't work. The theory is flawed because it ignores the fact that the only reason you smoke in the first place is because you're hooked on the drug. Continue taking the drug and you will remain hooked. You will continue to see the cigarette as a pleasure or crutch and you will convince yourself that you're making a sacrifice.

The popular substitute today is vaping. It's often the case that people who vape put more nicotine into their system than people who smoke. Smokers are limited by where and when they are allowed to smoke. Vaping does not have the same restrictions. With any addiction, the tendency is to do it more rather than less, which is why you see people vaping constantly. And have you noticed how the devices are getting bigger and bigger? Huge plumes of vapour doing who knows what harm? If you took away their vaping kit and offered them a cigarette, do you think they'd be able to refuse?

The use of substitutes to help people quit smoking is a clear case of a solution to a problem that doesn't exist. The problem for smokers is that they're hooked on nicotine. You can't get unhooked by taking more nicotine. The only way to free yourself from the slavery of smoking is to stop taking the nicotine and stop believing that smoking gives you pleasure or a crutch.

People who quit smoking this way find it easy to quit and stay free because they don't see it as giving up. They don't feel deprived, and so they don't mope. From the moment they unravel the brainwashing and remove all desire for nicotine, they are free to get on with their lives as a happy non-smoker.

Easyway is a solution to a genuine problem. It works by helping people with addictions to change their mindset and challenge their beliefs. Whether or not you have any addictions, you should apply this principle to all your thoughts.

NINTH INSTRUCTION:
QUESTION EVERYTHING YOU'VE EVER BEEN TOLD
AND EVERYTHING YOU BELIEVE

Opening your mind means more than accepting new ideas – it means accepting that old ideas may also be false. Remember the table illusion in Chapter Four. It's very easy to believe illusions, but once you've seen through one and know the truth it's impossible to be fooled by it again.

This is how you can tell what is real and what is a myth. Question it, open your mind, and look at it through your own eyes and in the context of your own experience. Does it add up?

Most of us stumble through life believing just about everything we're told. We're not conditioned to question everything and that makes us easy bait for people who want to sell us things that are bad for us. Take a moment to question every piece of information that comes your way and you will develop a much clearer view of how things really are.

A PROBLEM SHARED

You've heard the expression "A problem shared is a problem halved". You've probably experienced this in action at some point in your life. It refers to the comforting feeling you get when you tell someone else about a problem. Simply by talking about it, the problem becomes much less severe in your mind. You stop worrying about it and find the inner strength to solve it.

Your problem is halved. So what happens to the other half? Does the person you shared it with take it on? The proverb might suggest that this is the case, but it isn't. In most instances the person you share your problem with is required to do nothing more than listen.

THE OTHER HALF OF YOUR PROBLEM DISAPPEARS BECAUSE IT DIDN'T EXIST IN THE FIRST PLACE

By talking about your problem, you are putting yourself in a position of awareness. While it's in your head, you are wrapped up in it and unable to see a way out. By describing it to someone else you are effectively forcing yourself to observe it as it really is and when you do that all of the imagined layers of anxiety fall away.

The same thing happens when you take a mindful approach to your thoughts. The mindfulness exercise replaces the need for a friend or confidant – you share your problem with yourself and in doing so you gain a realistic perspective on the situation.

CUTTING OUT THE NOISE IN THE NIGHT

As I've said many times, mindfulness is not about banishing thought, it's about being present with your thoughts and not letting them run away with you. The aim is to see things more clearly, to understand your thoughts and how they make you feel. When we do that we gain the full value of this incredible power, harnessing it rather than letting it run riot and driving us to distraction. The power is awareness. And consciousness.

We are so conditioned to spending our time finding solutions to problems that sometimes we feel uncomfortable when there are no problems in our minds. You can find yourself lying awake in the middle of the night and, rather than switch off and go back to sleep, you go looking for something to think about: that email you need to write tomorrow; some childcare that you need to sort out; ways of earning more money; whether or not you need to get the car serviced…

There's a sense of "I'm awake now, I might as well do something useful with my time." All you're doing is filling your mind with thoughts, which then go round and round without resolution because you're not in a position to act on them.

Uncontrolled thinking is at its worst in the middle of the night because you're helpless to do anything but think, and so you become more and more anxious. On top of the issues that you try to think through as you lie there in the dark is the added worry that you're losing sleep again and that this is becoming a habit. The thought of waking up in the night begins to worry you before you go to sleep.

The problem is that you see waking in the night as a threat and immediately go into panic mode as soon as it happens. You wake up with your head in the box of flies and start thrashing about, trying to fight the thoughts off. But being aware that you have this problem gives you the opportunity to solve it.

Before you go to sleep, accept that you are likely to wake up in the night. Rather than seeing this as another assault that will need to be tackled, think of the thoughts that are going to enter your mind as a kindly but slightly nagging Aunt Joan. She's not a threat and you don't have to deal with her when she wakes you in the night.

Then, when you do wake up, your first reaction won't be panic and annoyance with yourself; it will be a kinder acceptance that Aunt Joan is paying a visit. Listen to what she has to say, thank her for any useful reminders, and then let her go. There is no need to act on Aunt Joan's comments now. Relax and go back to sleep.

The more you practise this mindful approach to waking in the night, the easier it will become. You will get a better night's sleep, which in turn will leave you less stressed, more energetic, and better able to deal with the issues raised by Aunt Joan when you have the opportunity to do so. Over time, Aunt Joan's visits will become less frequent because you're less anxious going to sleep at night and your mind is no longer conditioned to waking up and whirring.

LETTING GO OF THE STRUGGLE

The more you grapple with the flies buzzing around your head, the louder the buzz. When you let go of the struggle, the buzz quietens. The problems may still be there, but you are not stuck on them. You can observe them from a position of objectivity and see them as they really are.

Cutting out the noise does not necessarily mean leading a quiet life. Taking a mindful approach to life does not mean living away from it all and cutting yourself off from the hustle and bustle of modern life. That is not our aim. The aim of this book is to help you find happiness in whatever sort of life you want to pursue.

Some people love noise and feel anxious when things are too quiet. This is a method for getting more out of life, however you choose to lead it. It's absolutely fine to lead a busy, vibrant, exciting life. The point is that whatever lifestyle you prefer, it will be better if you have a clear head, free from buzzing thoughts and anxieties.

By being able to clear your mind from the noise of anxious thoughts, you will be better equipped to:

MAKE GOOD DECISIONS

TAKE POSITIVE ACTIONS

MAKE SOUND JUDGMENTS

HEAR WHAT'S REALLY GOING ON

BE HAPPY

EXERCISE: MINDFUL LISTENING

This is a powerful exercise for bringing your full attention to sounds and listening. It can be done as a formal seated practice or when walking (see next chapter), or as an exercise in paying attention when someone is talking.

To absolutely listen to someone, without getting hooked into a thought about how you are going to reply, is an art worth practising. To know you have been heard is also a joy and can improve relationships both at home and in the workplace.

Practise really listening to your friends and family, especially children. Get into the habit of putting your phone to one side when a child enters the room. Look them in the eye and listen to not only what they are saying, but the emotion around what is being said too. Reflect back to them what they have said, so they feel that they have been heard and have the opportunity to correct something if you haven't heard it as they intended.

When you are doing any of the exercises in this book, or any other mindfulness practice you might come across elsewhere, sounds should not be a distraction. Sounds are all part of the present moment and if you regard a sound as noise, it's because the sounds are being resisted.

1. Get into a comfortable position. If you are seated, make sure your feet are both placed on the floor, feeling the contact of your feet on the floor, and place cushions behind your back if necessary to make your posture more comfortable.

2. Relax your hands in your lap and then gently become aware of your breathing as you start to follow your breath in and out. Take a few deep breaths to begin with, breathing way down into your belly area, and following it as your breath rises and falls with its natural rhythm.

3. Now try bringing your attention to the sounds where you are, the sounds close by, really bringing your absolute attention to the sounds and focusing on them completely. Allow any thoughts, emotions, or feelings to arise and pass, and just bring yourself back to the sounds.

4. Now take your attention a bit further afield, to the sounds further away, really listening and focusing on the sounds in the distance. Watch how your mind wants to label them, but try accepting the sounds as they are, as they appear, with no judgment and no

labelling – just listening – just being present to the sounds. Again, allow thoughts to arise and come back to the sounds.

5. Now see if you can open up your hearing to ALL the sounds you can hear, close by and far away. It can seem like there is an orchestra of sounds out there – open your hearing, your listening, to the vast collection of sounds and be present with them all.

6. Gently bring your attention back to the sounds close by, the sounds really close to you – maybe the sound of your breath as your body breathes for you. Focus now just on your breath, the rise and fall of your natural breath, allowing thoughts, feelings, and emotions to arise and pass, bringing your attention to your breath. And now gently open your eyes and stretch.

SUMMARY

- Free yourself from the tug-of-war of fear by addressing the genuine threat

- NINTH INSTRUCTION: QUESTION EVERYTHING YOU'VE EVER BEEN TOLD AND EVERYTHING YOU BELIEVE

- A problem observed is a problem halved

- Go to sleep prepared to be woken

- Cutting out the noise doesn't mean living a quiet life – just a happy one

CHAPTER 15
RECONNECT

IN THIS CHAPTER
• RECONNECT WITH REALITY • RECONNECT WITH YOUR PHYSICAL SELF
• EXERCISE: MINDFUL WALKING
• BODY AND MIND IN HARMONY • RIDING THE CHANGES

One of the great things about your capacity for thought is that it enables you to project into the future and revisit the past. You can learn the lessons of past experience, and from other people's experience, and use them to plan for a better future. The one thing that gets overlooked, however, is the present.

When you are wrapped up in thought, you are not paying attention to what is going on in the present. The wandering mind tends to focus on past regrets and future anxieties. You now have the knowledge and techniques to detach from thought when you feel your mind wandering into negativity and bring your awareness back to what's happening now.

If you're still finding it hard to control your wandering mind, practise the counting the breath exercise in Chapter 7. The more you practise, the easier it becomes. As thoughts arise, bring the count back to 1, refocus and count to 10. This will help you to develop the ability to detach from your thoughts whenever you become aware of them carrying you away into negativity.

RECONNECT WITH REALITY

Being present with experience as it happens gives you a more accurate perspective on how things really are. When you allow your imagination to create your world, you end up with a disconnection between reality and your perception of reality. This is where anxiety takes hold. By mulling over past experiences and fretting about the future, you miss out on what is real – what is happening here and now.

It's a different part of your brain that deals with real experiences, the part that picks up signals from your senses. When you are wrapped up in thought, this part of the brain becomes subjugated and you become oblivious to much of what is actually going on around you.

Most people who drive cars will know the sensation of not being able to remember the last few minutes of driving. Clearly their senses were working because they've succeeded in staying on the road perfectly safely and not crashing into anything, yet they paid no conscious attention to their senses during that time because they were lost in thought. They have no recollection of the sounds or sights they must have experienced in those few minutes.

This doesn't mean they were driving dangerously. The mind is very clever in the way it can continue to carry out complex tasks like controlling a car while focusing your thoughts on something else altogether. But this just shows how we can become oblivious to reality when we're lost in thought.

It also shows that thought is not reality. While you're lost in thought, reality is constantly changing.

What's happening in reality can be both good and bad. The

important thing is that you are aware of it and accept it with kindness.

You can practise developing your perception of reality with a mindful eating exercise, as described in Chapter One. Eating is a classic example of an activity we carry out without awareness. With mindful eating, you take the time to appreciate every aspect of the food, from its appearance and feel in your hand to the taste and texture of it in your mouth. You notice details and sensations that normally pass you by when you eat.

The result is a much richer sensory experience that creates a stronger connection between body and mind. This makes you better equipped to face unpleasant experiences and sensations, such as pain, and hold them in perspective, rather than weaving a calamitous scenario around them. This acceptance of difficulty takes the energy out of your reaction and thus reduces your stress.

RECONNECT WITH YOUR PHYSICAL SELF

The more connected you are with the sensations of your body, the more clarity you will have as to who you really are, what you really want, and what you're really capable of. It helps to remove any fixed identities that can lead you into negative behaviour.

The body scan, as described in Chapter Five, is a great exercise for developing a stronger connection with physical sensations. Try to get into the routine of practising the body scan every night before you go to sleep, or every morning when you wake up. It's good practice for coming out of thought and tuning in to your senses.

You will notice feelings of pleasure and pain. There is no need to do anything about them. Simply hold them in awareness, noticing how they change constantly and the thoughts they give rise to. If you notice your thoughts running away with you in search of solutions, gently bring them back to focus.

When you're out and about too, pay attention to the physical sensations you experience in any given situation. How do you respond to feelings like temperature, sound, sight, smell, and taste? Make a point of not letting experiences pass you by without you noticing how your body reacts.

EXERCISE: MINDFUL WALKING

Walking is a wonderful way to take exercise, free your mind, and remove stress. It has been shown to be conducive to conversation because we find talking side-by-side less challenging than talking face to face. The rhythmic movement of arms and legs helps to free the mind – a lot of people like to do their thinking while walking because they find a greater clarity and objectivity.

Walking takes the mind into a deeper sensory space where the distractions of anxious thought are replaced by a more focused, creative mental process. It helps to lift you out of your thoughts and heightens your perception. The further you walk, the more you begin to notice the things that are happening around you. This exercise is designed to get you noticing from the moment you set off.

1. Begin by standing up as straight and tall as you can

and notice the feelings in your body. Are you feeling nimble or a bit stiff? Do your legs feel heavy or light? Notice your posture and deportment. Now begin to walk with a steady rhythm, perhaps slightly slower than you normally walk, but still at a pace that's comfortable for you. Notice the feeling of your feet meeting the ground.

2. As you walk, spend the next 30 seconds or so paying attention to what you can see going on around you. Notice the people, the cars, the buildings, trees, and birds. See how people are moving, the colours they're wearing, the shapes of things. If you're in the countryside and there are no other people or traffic, notice the stillness, but remember there is never nothing going on. Look for the small signs of activity – an insect on a leaf, for example. Accept all these sights into your consciousness without any judgment. Just acceptance.

3. Now turn your attention towards sounds alone for 30 seconds. If you're near traffic, just be careful to notice roads, crossings, and other potential hazards. What can you hear and how does it make you feel? Car engines? Birdsong? A distant farm vehicle? Children coming out of school? Footsteps? Try not to think about where these noises are coming from, just be aware of them, and tune in to the sounds.

4. For the next 30 seconds turn your attention to the smells that are reaching your nostrils. Notice how these smells trigger thoughts and memories – smell is the most evocative of all our senses – and how your mind begins to conjure up a story around them. Just bring your mind gently back to the rhythm of your walking.

5. Now focus on physical feelings for 30 seconds. Be aware of your leg muscles driving you along, your feet making contact with the ground, and your arms swinging by your sides. Is it warm or cold? Is it raining or dry? Windy or calm? There's no need to get wrapped up in these sensations – just notice them and the way they come and go in consciousness. If your mind begins to wander, bring it gently back to focus on the rhythm of walking.

6. Now allow your focus to turn to whatever sensations you like. Notice how your mind reacts to whatever comes up. You should be highly aware now of the life going on around you. Even if you're somewhere very serene, you will notice the movements of nature taking place within that serenity. Be aware of how these things make you feel as they come and go.

Mindful walking is a great exercise for any type of walk. If you have a regular short walk that you take, to work or to the shops for example, plan it so that you can divide the time up according to the stages set out above. This will help you to connect with your physical self, with the present and with reality.

BODY AND MIND IN HARMONY

There is a strong connection between physical and mental wellbeing. The one feeds the other. When you are not connected with the sensations in your body, problems arising will cause mental trauma without you realizing why. Similarly, if you obsess about every physical ache and pain you will put yourself under unnecessary mental stress, which in turn will have a detrimental effect on you physically.

But when you connect with your senses mindfully, you create a powerful bond between body and mind that benefits you in the following ways:

AWARENESS THAT THINGS ARE CONSTANTLY CHANGING, WHICH HELPS YOU TO BECOME UNSTUCK FROM FIXED IDEAS

APPRECIATION OF THE INCREDIBLE MACHINE THAT YOU ARE, WHICH HELPS YOU TO BUILD SELF-ESTEEM AND CONFIDENCE

ABILITY TO OBSERVE WITHOUT JUDGMENT AND TO ACCEPT RATHER THAN AVOID CHALLENGING EXPERIENCES

***ELEVATION FROM THE FRENZY OF THOUGHT TO
A DETACHED, OBJECTIVE VIEWPOINT OFFERING A
MORE REALISTIC PERSPECTIVE***

EXPERTISE IN PAYING ATTENTION

RIDING THE CHANGES

All of these benefits add up to a two-fold overall benefit of
reducing your perceived threats to their real size and, at the
same time, making you more resilient to deal with them. Just as
stress and anxiety make problems look bigger than they really
are in your mind and leave you feeling physically drained as
you remove the layers of anxiety through mindfulness, the
problems diminish and your physical strength increases.

As you remove the stress, other lifestyle improvements take
place without any effort. You sleep better, eat more healthily,
and feel more inclined to exercise. This gives you more energy
and a heightened sense of wellbeing, which in turn reduces
your stress further still.

Now when bad news comes your way, you're in a much
stronger condition to withstand it. You've reconnected with an
amazing power that lies dormant most of the time when you
spend your life wrapped in thought – the power of your body
and mind.

As the tide of life ebbs and flows and the occasional riptide
comes your way, you learn to accept it and ride it out, rather
than trying to fight it.

Skyscrapers are designed to sway with the wind. If they
weren't, they would crumble. Human beings are the same. We

are designed to bend not snap. If you find yourself snapping, then you've become disconnected somewhere along the line. Go back and re-read this chapter if any of this is not clear. Otherwise you're ready to start reversing the brainwashing that has led you away from mindfulness.

SUMMARY

- **Reconnect with the present when your mind wanders into regret or anxiety**

- **Reconnect with reality and reduce your stress**

- **Reconnect with your physical self and notice that everything is constantly changing**

- **Practise mindful walking**

- **Physical and mental wellbeing feed each other**

CHAPTER 16
REVERSE THE BRAINWASHING

IN THIS CHAPTER
• THINK DIFFERENTLY • THE TRUTH ABOUT MINDFULNESS
• TIME TO TAKE THE CONTROLS • EXERCISE: OBSERVING YOUR THOUGHTS

When you picked up this book, you may have been sceptical about mindfulness. Despite the fact that millions of people are now turning to mindfulness for help in coping with the stresses of modern life, the concept is still widely regarded with suspicion. There is an association with mysticism, religion, hippies, and cults, which is off-putting for a lot of people. The truth is that you can practise mindfulness in a multitude of ways, without any association with religion, cults, hippies, or mysticism. It's only brainwashing that makes anyone think otherwise. Those of us who live in the Western world have been conditioned to regard anything that challenges our normal way of thinking with suspicion.

Doesn't that strike you as odd? That a species with the incredible capacity for thought should impose restrictions on the way we think? It's a bit like being given a powerful sports car and only ever driving it in town at 30mph. If you had a powerful sports car, would you be sceptical about taking it out on to the open road and seeing what it could do? Would you be afraid of what lies out there beyond the city limits?

Of course you wouldn't. The whole point of owning a sports car is to take it out, explore its limits, and enjoy the thrill of driving it at full power.

The same applies to your brain. Most people go through life without ever exploring the full power of their mind. From the moment we are born, we are conditioned to follow the flock and we grow up with a fear of finding ourselves separated, even when we can see the flock is being fed to the wolves.

Brainwashed into thinking that it's the right thing to do, we take on pressures and sacrifice happiness without stopping to question whether what we're being pressured into doing is really in our best interests. We follow the example of role models who appear to "have it all" and make ourselves miserable in the process. Somewhere deep down we know that the image presented by film stars, rock stars, and other celebrities is heavily airbrushed and that the truth behind the image is far from idyllic, yet we still allow ourselves to be drawn to the light like moths to a flame.

We are taken in by advertising, promising us a life of beauty and affluence. These influencers prey on our fears around money, acceptance, and health. Every day we are bombarded with messages that trigger our most fundamental anxieties.

"CAN I AFFORD IT?"

"AM I ATTRACTIVE?"

"AM I GOING TO DIE?"

These are the anxieties behind all our obsessions and fears. We are sold a picture of who we should be and how we should live, then made to feel anxious that we can't. Rather than challenging these ideas, we assume life has to be like this.

WE DON'T THINK FOR OURSELVES

Perhaps you challenge that statement. You make dozens of choices every day, right? What brands of food to buy, which utility company to go with, what credit card to have, which route to drive, what to watch or listen to, what to wear, who to see... Sure, there are countless choices to be made, but how often do you choose something that's completely alien to you?

A good analogy is the Indian restaurant menu. The average menu in an Indian restaurant offers an incredible choice of dishes. You sit down and scan through them, mulling over the choices and discussing the various descriptions with your companions. And then what do you plump for?

THE SAME DISH THAT YOU ALWAYS HAVE

Okay, there may be three or four dishes that you always choose between, but you're still not exploring the whole menu. Not even close. And the choices you make in other aspects of life are similarly restricted to what you know and feel comfortable with.

THINK DIFFERENTLY

This human tendency to stick to the familiar makes it very easy for advertisers, politicians, and other influencers to control our behaviour. We're so predictable that they categorize us all into "demographic groups" and tailor their messages accordingly.

The idea that mindfulness is something peculiar that is practised by peculiar people is a typical piece of misinformation put about by influencers who want to keep us in those predictable mainstream groups. It's not in their interests for us to think for ourselves. Like all their other brainwashing, this false impression of mindfulness has been lapped up by mainstream society and that's why it is widely regarded with suspicion.

Why do we trust one source of information and not another? Quite simply, because it's different from what we're used to.

We are comfortable with our familiar assumptions. When they are challenged, we feel threatened and pull them closer to us. We choose to be brainwashed because that's what makes us feel comfortable.

But it doesn't make us happy. In fact, it makes us miserable, constantly preying on our fears, making us strive to fit in. This is where the brainwashing has got us. Look at the major trends in society today: there is an epidemic of obesity and Type 2 diabetes caused by bad diet; there is a global debt crisis; gambling and drug addiction are more prevalent than at any other stage in history. The one thing that is not on the rise is happiness.

Our brainwashed assumptions drive us to find happiness outside ourselves. Smoking, drinking, gambling, eating, and spending are all sold to us as ways to find happiness, but anyone who has got hooked on any of these things knows that they bring nothing but misery.

I call them false pleasures – they don't deliver happiness, but we're brainwashed into thinking that's our fault. When the novice smoker takes his first puff and finds it disgusting, he doesn't think it's a problem with the cigarette, he thinks it's a problem with himself. Rather than leave it alone, he keeps going, trying to get that pleasure that he's been told the cigarette will give him, inadvertently falling deeper and deeper into the trap. This is how addiction takes hold.

When you consider all the misery that your brainwashed assumptions cause, doesn't it make sense that a different way of thinking is exactly what you should be looking for? Rather than assume that all the stresses and anxieties that you battle with day by day are a sign of a weakness, get it clear in your mind:

IT'S NOT YOUR FAULT

Like everyone else, you have been conditioned from birth to follow assumptions that don't lead to happiness. The fact that you are reading this book shows that you have the awareness to seek a solution. Mindfulness is the solution.

THE TRUTH ABOUT MINDFULNESS

Practising mindfulness does not mean choosing one belief over another. Mindfulness is not about filling your mind with rules and assumptions, it's about freeing your mind and tapping in to your ability to make your own judgments.

MINDFULNESS GIVES YOU CHOICE

You may have heard people dismiss mindfulness as the latest fad, such is its recent boom in popularity, but there is nothing new about mindfulness.

As a recognized practice, it has been with us for thousands of years, but in truth it has existed since the evolution of mankind.

Our hectic, stress-filled lifestyle *is* something new. It's only very recently that society in general has felt so time-poor that there is no time to sit in quiet contemplation. The belief that a second spent doing nothing is a second wasted is a very new concept. We define ourselves by what we do rather than who we are, so we try to fill every available second with some sort of "doing".

The practice of mindfulness teaches us the value of "non-doing". We learn that there is never "nothing" going on; there is always something to observe, listen to, smell, taste, or feel. And when we spend our lives in the constant pursuit of doing, we miss out on these sensations and become disconnected from reality.

Neither is there anything weird about mindfulness. It's more natural than the mainstream way of thinking, which effectively allows other people to do your thinking for you. Surely that's weird. When you're given something as powerful as the human brain, why would you only use a small part of it?

That small part, intellect, should not be allowed to overrule your senses. Your senses are nature's design for perceiving what's really going on around you. When you allow your intellect to disconnect from your senses, it's like flying a plane on autopilot. There is no scope for flexibility and adaptation as the world around you changes; you act according to a pre-programmed set of rules that is not always appropriate for your circumstances.

Practising mindfulness is like switching your mind from autopilot to manual.

TIME TO TAKE THE CONTROLS

As you practise the mindfulness exercises in this book, you will notice your mindset changing from one of following to one of control. Mindfulness puts you back in charge and that's a feeling that breeds confidence. Much of the stress we suffer in life is caused by a feeling of powerlessness. As we begin to reconnect with our full potential as human beings, we feel empowered to handle challenges that previously would have overwhelmed us.

Just by getting into the habit of questioning everything, you start to see through the illusions. Whereas before you might have eaten a cake and assumed that it tasted good, taking the trouble to really taste the cake will replace assumption with truth. You might decide that the cake does taste good, or you might find that it's really just a mass of flavourless fat and flour, laced with sugar – either way it will be your decision. You will have taken control.

When you see the truth for yourself, you can't be fooled into believing the opposite. And so you start to build up a more complete picture of things as they really are. This puts you in a position of strength when it comes to making decisions. Not only are you basing your decisions on fact, you *know* you're basing your decisions on fact, which removes a major stress.

This is why it's important to question everything, especially if it's a source of stress or misery. Ask yourself, "What do I really think? What are my instincts telling me?" Mindfulness puts you more in tune with your instincts, more connected to physical sensations and thus better able to receive genuine signals from your senses that give you a realistic perception of experiences.

As you begin to approach experiences mindfully, you will come to regard this capacity for perception as second nature. In fact, it's first nature. We are all born with this instinctive ability and indeed we rely on it as infants, but it is squashed out of us as we grow up and become bombarded by brainwashing.

The principles of Easyway are one application of mindfulness and the results the method has achieved in helping people to quit smoking, drinking, and other addictions show just how effective and empowered humans can be when we reconnect all the parts of the incredible machine.

However sceptical you may be at the start, simply by practising mindfulness and following the instructions of Easyway you will discover for yourself that the method works. Provided you follow all the instructions, you cannot fail to reverse the brainwashing and free your mind to see things as they really are.

EXERCISE: OBSERVING YOUR THOUGHTS

This exercise can be added as an extension to the mindful listening exercise in Chapter 14. Follow the steps for mindful listening and, when you've finished the cycle of listening far and near, turn your attention to thoughts.

This is a great way of encouraging distance between you and your thoughts following meditation, and it also teaches you not to trust random thoughts. You soon begin to understand how your minds whirls around, always trying to plan ahead and anticipate problems. This meditation works best when it lasts for at least 20 minutes.

It can be done walking, sitting, standing or lying down.

After expanding your awareness of sounds and listening, we come back to breathing. Follow the natural rhythm of the breath – don't force it, just follow it. As you do so, allow thoughts, feelings, and emotions to arise and pass; it might help to see them as clouds passing by, before returning to your breathing. Sometimes it helps to imagine you are in a theatre, with the very best seat in the house and a perfect view of the stage. From this position, you can begin to observe your thoughts playing out on stage. Maybe they are putting on quite a show, but you are able to observe them without getting hooked into them – just observing them from a distance, not judging or questioning them. Observe them as you would your favourite TV show. Maybe the stage is quite empty, or perhaps a crowded scene is playing out before your eyes. Whatever the scene, your job is just to observe. You might even hear some whispering in the wings – just bring this into your awareness, into your vision. There is really very little to do but sit back and watch the show. If you find yourself on stage interacting, maybe dancing with a thought, then gently, and with friendliness, make your way back to your seat and continue to observe. Each time a thought presents itself on stage, observe it – after a while, you may want to check your posture. If you are sitting in a chair, make sure your feet are placed securely on the ground. Check that you are not slumping, that your shoulders are relaxed, and that you are seated gracefully with a straight back and long spine, continuing to watch the show in all its splendour. The point is to observe your mind and thoughts from a distance, and remain in your seat. If you find you have wandered up on to the stage, then it's a matter of simply returning back to where you were sitting. To bring the meditation to an end, slowly rock from side to side, softly opening your eyes, and then mindfully moving on to your next activity.

SUMMARY

- **Explore the full power of your brain**
- **Be prepared to think differently**
- **Mindfulness gives you choice**
- **Switch your mind to manual**
- **Simply by practising mindfulness, your mindset will change**

CHAPTER 17
MINDFULNESS AND ADDICTION

IN THIS CHAPTER
• CLOSING THE VOID • EASYWAY IN A NUTSHELL
• FACING THE PROBLEM, NOT USING WILLPOWER

Even if you feel you don't have any addictions, I recommend that you read this chapter to arm yourself against the possibility of becoming addicted in future and to have an understanding of how it works with others.

In Chapter 4, I explained how addiction relies on brainwashing to trap its victims in a downward spiral. We are all, addicts and non-addicts alike, subjected to brainwashing throughout our lives and the brainwashing that surrounds addictive activities like smoking, drinking, and gambling is particularly intense. It's enough to lure the most strong-willed of people into the trap and once you're in the trap it convinces you that your deadliest enemy is your best friend.

People with addictions live with lots of assumptions that keep them trapped. In the case of nicotine, for example, it is widely assumed that smoking helps you concentrate, relaxes you, calms your nerves, makes you look cool, gives you confidence in social situations, and helps you keep your weight down. All of these assumptions are complete nonsense, but they are put about by a variety of sources, from tobacco advertisers right across to anti-smoking campaigners, and such is the ingenious nature of addiction that when you're in the trap, you perceive them to be real.

Nicotine addiction is a major cause of distraction. When you're waiting for your next fix, it's almost impossible to concentrate on anything else. That's why people who smoke believe that smoking helps them to concentrate, because when they light up they are no longer distracted by the craving for their next fix. What they fail to realize is that smoking was destroying their concentration in the first place.

The same process applies to relaxing, calming your nerves, and feeling confident in social situations. The reality of these situations is that when you have to go without your little crutch, it sets your nerves on edge; you feel anxious, irritable, and insecure. As soon as you take a drag on a cigarette, the restlessness is partially relieved, and so you are fooled into believing that the cigarette has relaxed you, calmed you, and given you confidence. In other words, you light the cigarette to feel like a non-smoker. It just partially relieves the discomfort caused by the addiction.

Smoking is perceived as cool because over the years, even recently, tobacco companies have made use of famous role models to promote their products, whether in advertisements or via product placement in films and television. Tobacco advertising is strictly regulated these days, but there are still plenty of famous actors and actresses smoking on screen.

What the glossy images don't show is the yellow fingers, the stained teeth, grey skin, and bad breath. Directors don't include endless bouts of coughing and wheezing in their scenes. We don't see these smoking role models going into hospital to have limbs removed or being told they've got only a few months to live.

The reality of smoking is definitely not cool and thankfully the number of people in Western society who smoke has been falling, thanks in no small part to Easyway live seminars, online seminars, and books which are estimated to have helped more than 30 million smokers to freedom.

Then there are the people who are afraid to quit smoking because they think they'll put on weight. The only reason smoking is perceived as a method for losing weight is because the pangs caused by nicotine withdrawal feel similar to hunger. People who try to quit with the withdrawal method become very aware of the pangs and try to satisfy them by eating. Not surprisingly they put on weight after they've quit.

You're actually more likely to put on weight when you smoke because you are constantly feeling that craving sensation, and so you feel like you're permanently hungry. With genuine hunger, the craving stops when your hunger is satisfied. But if you smoke, you will continue to experience a pang that feels like hunger, and so you never get that feeling of satisfaction.

Of course, smokers think that smoking helps to suppress their appetite or speed up their metabolism to the extent of controlling their weight, but that's just part of the confidence trick. And whereas smoking does increase a smoker's metabolic rate, the suggestion that it does so to the extent that it burns hundreds of extra calories each day is simply wrong. There isn't some kind of super calorie-burning machine inside your body when you smoke.

If you know how hard, fast, and for how long you have to pedal on an exercise bike to burn off a few hundred calories, you won't find that hard to accept.

The false assumptions that enslave people with smoking and other addictions take hold because they are so widely accepted and the effect of addiction itself creates an illusion that appears to prove the assumptions true. Through mindfulness, you learn to question these assumptions and determine your own truth, by observing without judgment and developing the ability to see things as they really are.

CLOSING THE VOID

The disconnection between our assumptions and our experience leaves a void like a deep ravine, over which we hover with a sense of insecurity. Your faith in your parents, for example, is one case: as children, we trust our parents to look after us at all costs and to be unimpeachable in their behaviour. As we grow older we realize they are only human, capable of letting us down, sometimes betraying our trust, and leaving us vulnerable.

This and many other disillusionments add to the void as we grow up. We gradually learn that the world can be a cruel, uncaring place, unlike the safe, cosy world into which we were born, and our sense of insecurity increases.

We go in search of something to fill the void: idols, cigarettes, booze, food, shopping. But everything we put our faith in has the potential to let us down and open up the void again. Anything that's addictive leaves us feeling insecure as we withdraw from each fix, and so a new void opens up.

Through mindfulness, we learn to close the void between

expectation and experience by reconnecting with our senses, thus gaining a more accurate perception of reality. In other words, we stop deluding ourselves and start seeing things as they really are.

EASYWAY IN A NUTSHELL

My book, *The Easy Way to Stop Smoking*, promised to help people quit smoking easily and permanently without relying on willpower or having to go through a painful withdrawal period. For most smokers, this was revolutionary for four reasons:

THEY HAD ALWAYS ASSUMED THAT QUITTING WAS HARD

THEY HAD ALWAYS ASSUMED THAT QUITTING WAS RARELY PERMANENT

THEY HAD ALWAYS ASSUMED THEY WOULD NEED ALL THEIR WILLPOWER

THEY HAD ALWAYS ASSUMED THERE WOULD BE A PAINFUL WITHDRAWAL PERIOD

But my method was different from any other. Where other methods tried to help smokers resist the temptation to ever smoke again, Easyway removed the temptation altogether. And it proved incredibly successful. It did this not by helping smokers to summon the willpower to resist their desire to smoke but by helping them to unravel the brainwashing that made them think they wanted to smoke in the first place.

The first assumption it addressed was the reason people smoke. Ask smokers why they smoke and they will say things like "I like the taste," or, "I like the way it looks," or, "I find it relaxing." In fact, they smoke for one reason and one reason only:

ADDICTION

The only reason people start smoking is because they are brainwashed into thinking that it will provide them with some kind of pleasure or benefit or crutch, even something as banal as trying to look cool or fit in with the crowd or rebelling. The only reason they continue is because they get hooked on an addictive drug. Remove the addiction – and understand how the brainwashing works – and you stop smoking without any difficulty at all.

Smoking creates two monsters: the Little Monster in the body that lives on nicotine and cries out whenever the drug is withdrawing and it wants another fix; and the Big Monster in the brain that interprets the cries of the Little Monster as "I want a cigarette!" These monsters can be very disconcerting when you don't understand what they are. With Easyway's mindful approach, you learn to recognize the two monsters and hold them in awareness, rather than feeling that you have to fight them or give them what they want.

The Big Monster is created by the brainwashing. Without the Big Monster, the pangs of nicotine withdrawal are so tiny as to be almost imperceptible. The task, therefore, is to kill the Big Monster by unravelling the brainwashing. You can then stop smoking and leave the Little Monster to die in its own time. Those terrible withdrawal pains that smokers are so afraid of turn out to be nothing more than the feeble cries of the Little Monster in its death throes. Without the Big Monster to interpret those cries as "I want a cigarette", and to create an ever-growing feeling of deprivation, they are barely noticeable.

So we unravel the brainwashing by addressing the myths that have been built up around smoking: the myths to do with concentration, relaxation, stress relief, socializing, weight control, looking cool, and all the others. By approaching these myths mindfully, rather than assuming them to be true, we quickly see the flaws in the smoking argument. More than that, we see that the opposite is true in every case.

SMOKING DOESN'T RELAX YOU; IT STOPS YOU RELAXING

SMOKING DOESN'T AID CONCENTRATION; IT DESTROYS IT

SMOKING DOESN'T CALM YOUR NERVES; IT PUTS YOU PERMANENTLY ON EDGE AND INCREASES STRESS

SMOKING DOESN'T LOOK COOL; IT LOOKS AND SMELLS DISGUSTING

Addiction traps its victims into believing in the illusion of pleasure. It's a simple but ingenious trick. First it creates discomfort as the drug withdraws, then offers some relief with the next fix, thereby creating the impression that the drug has given some sort of pleasure or crutch. It's the equivalent of wearing tight shoes all day, just for the relief of taking them off.

Easyway teaches you to see the illusion of pleasure for what it really is. Once you see through the illusion, you can't be fooled by it again.

As well as removing the illusion of pleasure, the mindful approach of Easyway helps to remove the fear of quitting by showing that you are not "giving up" anything. You learn to see that the myths are false, smoking does nothing for you, and so there is no sacrifice, nothing to mope for when you quit. In fact, you have marvellous gains to look forward to.

The final assumption to remove is that timing can affect how easy it is to quit. For example, the springboard of New Year's Eve or a summer holiday. But the point is that, with Easyway, quitting is easy at any time because you are left with no lingering desire to smoke. Therefore, the best time to quit is NOW!

All smokers want to quit. They only pretend they're happy smoking because they feel stupid and helpless in the trap and don't want to admit to that. Give them the key to walk out of their prison and none of them would choose to stay inside. Easyway provides the key with a series of simple instructions. All you have to do is follow all the instructions in order and you cannot fail to escape.

There is no need to wait for anything. You are free the moment you unravel the brainwashing and remove the desire to smoke. The ritual of the "final cigarette" confirms everything you have learned about smoking, through mindfully observing your thoughts and assumptions and seeing things as they really are. Many people are so ready to quit that they don't want to smoke the final cigarette which is the climax of the method. They have already experienced a moment of revelation when they realize that they are free; they no longer have any desire to smoke.

It takes a few days for the last traces of nicotine to leave the body and the Little Monster to die but, free from the misconceptions about smoking, it's actually a period of great satisfaction and enjoyment. Free from the Big Monster, the feeble cries of the Little Monster are no threat at all, but a happy reminder that you're destroying your deadly enemy.

Unlike people who quit with the willpower method, there is no feeling of deprivation, and so no conflict of the will. You can relax and get on with enjoying life as a happy non-smoker straight away.

This, in short, is how I set about curing the world of smoking and developed a method that not only helped millions of smokers to quit, but has also helped people with other addictions. The method has achieved widespread success around the world because it works. And it works where most other methods fail because it approaches the problem mindfully.

Where other methods accept the assumptions that lead us into the addiction trap and try to give people the strength to overcome the desire, Easyway teaches you to examine those assumptions and apply your own mental processes to see the truth for yourself. In this way, those assumptions are shown to be false, and so the desire is removed.

FACING THE PROBLEM, NOT USING WILLPOWER

Mindfulness teaches us to hold difficulties like addiction in awareness without judging ourselves or feeling we have to grapple with the problem or avoid it. When we try to blot out threats and dangers, they appear bigger and scarier in our imagination. By accepting the existence of the problem and being present with it, we are able to keep it in proportion.

When we're told to use willpower, we are effectively encouraged to tackle problems by grappling with them, avoiding them, or thinking them through. As I have explained throughout the book, that approach only leads to more stress and makes the problem appear bigger and scarier than it really is.

The key to Easyway, and mindfulness in general, is seeing things as they really are. When we see problems as a struggle, we add layers of difficulty and stress and make the problems worse. When we let go of the struggle, problems diminish and the knots unravel.

SUMMARY

- **Mindfulness helps you see through the myths that fuel addiction**

- **Mindfulness helps to close the void between perception and experience**

- **Quitting any addiction is only hard if you use the wrong method**

- **Mindfulness enables you to face difficulties and keep them in proportion**

CHAPTER 18
CHOOSE HAPPINESS

IN THIS CHAPTER
• BEING PREPARED • READY NOT TO STRUGGLE
• RELEASE YOUR GRIP ON NEGATIVITY

"Most folks are about as happy as they make their minds up to be."

Abraham Lincoln

Among the cynics who scoff at the idea that happiness is a choice we can all make, there is a sense that mindfulness somehow creates an illusion of happiness in its exponents by wiping their mind of unpleasant thoughts and that it's not genuine happiness. They believe that to experience genuine happiness you have to suffer first. Mindfulness, they say, is just a form of brainwashing that leaves people wandering around like spaced-out zombies with vacant grins on their faces.

This assumption could not be further from the truth. It's an example of how our brainwashed minds make up false scenarios to justify warped beliefs.

Studies have shown that people who are well practised at mindfulness are more alert, more responsive, more energetic, more astute, and more receptive to experiences. In other words, mindfulness does not anaesthetize but heightens sensory perception and leads to a more tuned-in connection with reality. You could call it an open mind.

As you become more receptive through mindfulness, you develop a greater awareness of the good things in life and happiness flows in.

That doesn't mean you are immune to suffering. You will still face pressure, pain, and misfortune from time to time; the difference is that with mindfulness you become better equipped to handle them. You learn to see that what happens and how you respond to it are two separate things.

BEING PREPARED

Often the biggest stresses in life are those that occur without warning. We're not ready for them, so we react as we would if a tiger leapt out from behind a tree. The element of surprise triggers the instinctive responses of fight, flight, or freeze, all of which are highly stressful.

When the surprise is not a tiger but something more commonplace like a phone ringing or a worrying thought entering your head, then the panic response is clearly an overreaction and the stress it causes is unnecessary. You can mitigate such overreactions simply by being prepared for the shock and having a plan in place.

In Chapter 14, we looked at the very common problem of being woken in the night by your own anxious thoughts and slipping straight into panic mode. The very act of waking in the night becomes a source of anxiety in itself, and so you go to sleep full of dread. You can remove that dread by going to bed with a different mindset, e.g. personifying the voices that wake you as the clucking Aunt Joan rather than a serious threat. By taking a more benign approach to being woken, you defuse the panic. You can then calmly accept the points that Aunt Joan wants to make without feeling that you have to deal with them right away.

The effect is a completely different attitude to waking in the night. You no longer regard the initial awakening as a dreaded precursor to hours of restlessness and another poor night's sleep. By removing that stress, you are able to take a calmer, more mindful approach to the thoughts in your head, accepting them without judgment and letting them go. Now you can relax and go back to sleep.

As we've mentioned, fear can be a source of severe anxiety or it can be a source of fun. It all depends how we perceive the cause. Our ability to handle fear when we're prepared is demonstrated by our reaction to the rides at a theme park. We put ourselves through extreme fear when we go on a rollercoaster, for example – that's the whole point of the ride – but because we are prepared for it the fear does not leave us feeling stressed and miserable. On the contrary, the feeling is one of elation.

READY NOT TO STRUGGLE

Being prepared is the first step in protecting yourself against negative thoughts. The next step is to have a method ready.

As you practise your mindfulness exercises, you will build up your ability to approach thoughts without become entangled in them. When you wake up in the night, for example, and the worries come into your mind, they don't panic you and you

The Wheel of Mindfulness

The Wheel of Mindfulness shows that when we allow ourselves to be distracted by the past/the future/egotism, etc., it leads to anxiety, stress, guilt, and other problems. We must find our way to the heart of the circle where freedom and peace of mind lie.

don't feel compelled to do something about them. Instead, you know that by observing them with a feeling of kindness you will be able to remain detached from any negative thoughts as they pass through your brain, without having to hide from them.

By mindfully observing and then letting go of anxious thoughts, you relieve yourself of their excess baggage and unburden yourself of the struggle. Free from the extra stress, you find yourself better prepared to accept difficulty and less worn down by anxiety.

Very quickly you can reverse the vicious circle of anxiety, tiredness, and stress and turn it into a positive cycle of mindfulness, energy and happiness.

Brainwashing is largely responsible for the prevalence of stress and anxiety in our modern way of life. Plugged into a fixed way of thinking that tells us we need to prove ourselves

Allen Carr's Easyway

Allen Carr's Easyway helps us recognize the misconceptions that prevent us from seeing the truth, and thus we can eliminate destructive behaviour. By freeing ourselves from illusions, we are taken back to the centre – to happiness and freedom.

through the things we do, rather than by being the people we are, we are drawn into believing that the path to happiness is through removing all problems, whether by fighting them off, pretending they don't exist, or thinking them through.

If we can't find happiness, we assume it's because we lack the fortitude to fight for it.

Mindfulness teaches us that striving or battling for happiness is a contradiction and that we only truly get somewhere by not trying to get anywhere. When you're caught up in the brainwashing, this seems counterintuitive, but as you make mindfulness a part of your life you see the logic in it everywhere.

Whether you regard life's stresses as a box of flies or a tangle of string, the same logic applies. You won't solve the problem through force or avoidance, and ruminating on it will only increase your stress. It's when you relax your grip that the string untangles; or when you lift your head out of the box of flies, the buzzing stops.

RELEASE YOUR GRIP ON NEGATIVITY

We've talked about how fixed identities become self-fulfilling. If you see yourself as weak-willed, unpopular, incapable, unlucky, etc., you will follow patterns of behaviour that confirm your self-image. A common identity that people get stuck with when they're stressed is:

"I CAN'T BE HAPPY"

Such is the brainwashing that you begin to believe that happiness is not an option, that life is about survival, meeting deadlines, paying bills, doing things for other people – as if all these things are, by their very nature, miserable. In reality, meeting deadlines, paying bills, and doing things for other people are hugely satisfying and can be a tremendous source of happiness. We only see them as a source of unhappiness if we approach them with a negative mindset. Then we convince ourselves that there's going to be a struggle and we feel threatened by them.

Some people go through life without ever feeling truly happy. That is a tragedy. The saddest thing of all is that they convince themselves that they don't have access to happiness – it's not for them. For whatever reason, they believe that suffering is their lot in life. If you think that applies to you, please get one thing clear in your mind:

YOU HAVE A RIGHT TO HAPPINESS

You also have the tools to achieve happiness. All you need is a method to unlock those tools. Mindfulness teaches us to unhook ourselves from fixed ideas and identities by recognizing the constant changes taking place and accepting that both good feelings and bad feelings will come and go and we don't have to attach ourselves to either.

Having learned how to free yourself from negative thoughts, you learn how to direct your focus towards positive experiences.

The positive effect of mindfulness on your connection with the world around you makes you more receptive to the incredible things that are taking place all the time. You begin to appreciate things that previously passed you by unnoticed and you effortlessly derive happiness from things you might have been cynical about before.

As you become more proficient at approaching your experiences mindfully, you will start to find that you can unhook your mind from automatic thoughts and assumptions and choose to focus on positive experiences. Or, put another way, you learn to choose happiness.

In Chapter One, I explained that happiness is an option, not a consequence of things that happen in life beyond your control. It's how you respond to the changing circumstances of life that determines whether you can be happy or not. And you *can* choose how you respond – all you need is a simple set of instructions to enable you to see that you have a choice.

By now, you should have learned enough about mindfulness to see that you *do* have a choice and you should be feeling excited about exercising that choice.

Perhaps you already are. What you are choosing is actually

the easier path in life – the one free from unnecessary stress, brainwashing, and illusions that leave you trapped in a vicious circle of unhappiness.

If you have any lingering doubts about any of the points we've covered, it's essential that you go back and read the relevant chapter again, so that you're absolutely clear about your right to happiness and your ability to turn your mindset towards a happy life.

If you have read and understood everything so far, you've followed all the instructions, and you can see everything clearly, you are ready for the final instruction.

TENTH INSTRUCTION: CHOOSE HAPPINESS!

SUMMARY

- **Mindfulness is not mind-numbing; it's mind-opening**

- **Bad experiences will happen – it's how you respond that makes the difference**

- **Prepare yourself for the difficulties that come your way**

- **With mindfulness, you know you have a method to cope**

- **Struggling for happiness is a contradiction**

- **You have a right to happiness**

- **You have the tools and you have a choice**

- **TENTH INSTRUCTION: CHOOSE HAPPINESS!**

CHAPTER 19
A MINDFUL LIFE

IN THIS CHAPTER
ENJOY DOING NOTHING • MINDFUL TECHNIQUES
• R.E.L.E.N.T • NORMAL SERVICE RESUMED •

The aim of this book is not just to give you a method for coping with stress, unwinding, and freeing your mind from anxiety, it is to open your eyes to the incredible power of the human body and mind and help you reconnect with your full potential, so you can lead a happy life, not dominated by fear, battered by stress, or worn down by endless rumination.

Once you have discovered the power of approaching life mindfully and begun to develop the techniques we've covered, you can begin to practise your new knowledge and skills in all sorts of everyday situations. The more you practise, the more your mind will become attuned, and soon you will find that it's the most natural thing in the world.

You can start having fun by practising mindfulness in your daily routines, situations in which you might previously have switched off or tried to occupy your mind with distractions. If you take the bus, train, or car to work, make a point of noticing everything that's going on around you. Pay attention to the person who sells you your ticket. Notice how they go through their routine, and how they have their task down to a fine art.

Listen to the sounds as you travel and notice how they come and go: voices, engine noises, horns, music, the squeaks and creaks of furniture... Take notice of the smells that arise and subside. If you're driving, feel the steering wheel in your hands and notice how it slides through your palms as you turn it.

The idea is to switch on to every detail, rather than switching off, which is what we normally do on the journey to work. We typically blot out everything that's going on and bury our heads in a book or music or some video on our phone. We assume that there's nothing going on worth noticing, but when you stop and pay attention you realize that there are countless things to observe.

Try the same approach when you're cooking dinner, eating, brushing your teeth, lying in the bath, or having a shower. Each of these activities involves myriad sensations that all stimulate the senses and heighten your perception of what's actually going on here and now. The more you practise tuning in, the more you train your brain to be alert to real life experience.

ENJOY DOING NOTHING

There is a general perception that life is more frenetic and stressful today than at any stage in history, and the blame falls squarely on one thing: the mobile phone. For many of us, these devices are the greatest technological breakthrough ever – which tends to overlook the train, the car, electric light, radio, television, the plane, satellite, keyhole surgery, etc., but that's by the by. Our phones provide us with the means to do just about everything we need to do from just about anywhere in the world, and that is pretty incredible.

However, mobile phones have changed our behaviour dramatically. Before they were invented, a walk to the shops would be a walk to the shops. Nowadays it's a phone call, a check of social media, a listen to music, a viewing of a video. Thanks to our phones, we fill every spare second with doing rather than just being.

We fill the minutes waiting for trains, buses, doctor's appointments, and haircuts by tuning in to our phones. When they first came along, it felt great no longer having to fill those dragging minutes watching the clock tick round, but now the phone comes out as a matter of routine and we occupy ourselves for the sake of it because of this obsession with *doing*.

The alternative to doing is *being*.

Being sees a different aspect of the brain at work – the sensory part that keeps you in touch with experience. Mindfulness develops this faculty, thus closing the void between thinking and sensing and removing the tension that arises when that void opens up.

Rather than taking out your phone whenever you have a few minutes to kill, practise some of the mindful techniques described in this book. Let go of the urge to use the time in achieving, and content yourself with just *being*. You will feel your mind relax like a muscle relaxing when you put down a heavy weight.

This practice helps to alter the perception that your thoughts are a complete picture of reality and opens your mind to the full range of sensations that make up the present moment. What you notice is that there is always something going on, something to observe and take interest in.

MINDFUL TECHNIQUES

There are many ways in which you can continue mindfulness practice after you finish this book. You can explore further forms of meditation and activities that embrace the principles of mindfulness, such as yoga, tai-chi, and hypnotherapy.

But the beauty of mindfulness is that you don't need to take up any specific activity or belief to make it part of your everyday lifestyle. As we've already mentioned, you can work it into the most routine activities, such as cooking, eating, and washing.

A simple but effective activity for practising mindfulness is walking. Walking is not only good for you physically; it also relaxes the mind, and leads to a state of detachment where you begin to forget about the self and experience life as a kind of alternative reality. This is not only relaxing but stimulating too. Rather than getting wrapped up in problems, as you do when you're inactive in bed at night, the effect of walking is to elevate your mind to a new perspective where sensory experience and conscious thought combine to provide clarity.

This heightened sensory experience is also evident when we challenge ourselves with creative activities, such as writing, playing sport, and music. With practice, we can take our mind to a place that seems to be almost out of body, where our achievements appear to happen without any conscious decision-making. In sport, they call it "the zone".

Socializing is conducive to happiness. It encourages a more healthy, outward-looking state of mind, as well as fostering behaviours that turn your attention towards the good things in life and free your mind from harmful constraints.

I have talked about the importance of noticing all the

good things in life. Friendships encourage us not only to feel gratitude but to express it. Regular expressions of gratitude have been shown to engender happiness and alleviate despair. Some people express their gratitude through prayer, others keep a gratitude journal or a gratitude jar, in which they make a point of writing something each day for which they're grateful. Every so often you open the journal or jar and remind yourself of all the reasons you have for being happy.

Being sociable also helps to remove resentment. Harbouring resentment and bitterness has a harmful effect on mental and physical health, while an outward-looking, sociable approach to life helps you to see the value of letting resentment go. If you feel resentful, mindfulness training will help you through a process of untangling yourself from the destructive negative thinking that you can remember with the word RELENT.

R	**Recognize** – accept that you are bearing a grudge
E	**Empathize** – try to see the situation from the other person's perspective
L	**Let go** – of the desire for retribution
E	**Enjoy** – the thought of life free from bitterness
N	**Name** – practise naming the other person with a feeling of kindness
T	**Talk** – get back on speaking terms as soon as you can

When you approach relationships mindfully, your inclination and ability to listen and empathize are enhanced. Your expectations are not guided by ego, but by a more rounded, objective perception. This in turn leads to greater understanding, a more selfless approach and happier relationships overall.

And happy relationships are a rich source of personal happiness. By letting something go (i.e. self-interest), you make a far more valuable gain (contentment).

NORMAL SERVICE RESUMED

After a period of applying mindfulness to your way of living you will have a moment when you realize that things have changed. Without having to make any strenuous effort, life has become easier, more relaxed, and more enjoyable. In short, you feel happier.

Through practising a different approach to the anxieties and difficulties that are an inevitable part of life, you have re-moulded your brain to work differently from the way you've been used to since childhood. This sounds like it should feel like a dramatic change, yet you hardly notice it happening for one very simple reason:

IT'S THE MOST NATURAL THING ON EARTH

The practice of mindfulness reconnects you with the full potential of nature's ingenious design for humankind. The techniques described in this book are not rocket science; they are techniques that we're all born with but lose touch with as we're bombarded by brainwashing.

The process of reconnecting is a marvellous, liberating

feeling and, when that moment comes and it dawns on you that the stress, anxiety, fear, struggling, and reaching out for artificial pleasures are no longer a dominant feature in your life, it's exhilarating.

The more you practise mindfulness, using whatever techniques you feel comfortable with, the more adept you will become. It's like working a muscle in a gym – regular, gentle repetition is all it takes to keep the muscle honed. There is no pain, no strenuous effort, nothing to give up – only marvellous gains to be made.

As well as working the muscle of mindfulness, the more you practise the more you will cleanse your mind of the pollution it's been exposed to from the day you were born. All that brainwashing built up through your life can take a while to wash away again, but once it's gone it's gone forever. You can never be fooled by those illusions again.

Of course, you need to be aware of new forms of brainwashing. The brainwashing doesn't stop happening, any more than the misfortune, pain, and pressure stop, and you will continue to be targeted by people who want you to see things a certain way. Remember the ninth instruction:

QUESTION EVERYTHING

Pay attention to what you're told and who is telling you. Avoid making assumptions based on other people's evidence. Tune in to your own experience and discover your own truth.

We are not promising that everything in life will be idyllic from now on. It's not realistic to expect to feel happy all the time. What is important is that the thought of unhappiness doesn't cause its own stress. Be prepared for the lows, resist the temptation to cling on to the highs, and accept that life requires a certain amount of rolling with the punches.

Throughout this book, I have tried to dispel the myth that mindfulness is just another form of brainwashing and to explain its principles in simple, down-to-earth terms that you can apply to every aspect of your life. I began with a question:

Imagine you could find a way to reduce the stress in your life, free yourself from anxiety, depression, and regret, and enjoy increased happiness and more peaceful relationships, while remaining calm and in control. Now imagine that, by achieving that happier mental state, you became less susceptible to sickness, injury, tiredness, and pain. If I told you that you have the power to achieve this happy state quickly, easily, and without making any sacrifices, how would you feel?

Mindfulness is nothing more or less amazing than the power to see things as they really are. We all have the ability to be mindful. We are all free to choose.

And that is the choice that you are making now. To apply the principles of mindfulness to all aspects of the rest of your life. It's like emerging from a dark, dusky, gloomy world of turmoil, confusion, anxiety, and depression, into a life of bright sunlight, happiness, calm, and contentment. Don't waste a moment more. You've arrived. Read through the chapter summaries that follow. Putting them into practice will ensure your success.

ENJOY THE REST OF YOUR LIFE!

SUMMARY

- Practise mindfulness in your everyday routines

- Resist the temptation to fill inactive time with doing

- Set yourself meaningful challenges and be sociable

- Never stop practising!

YIPPEE! YOU'RE FREE!

THE INSTRUCTIONS

1. FOLLOW ALL THE INSTRUCTIONS

2. BEGIN WITH A FEELING OF ELATION

3. OPEN YOUR MIND

4. PAY ATTENTION TO YOUR POSITIVE EXPERIENCES AS THEY OCCUR

5. WHENEVER YOU FEEL FEAR, QUESTION IT

6. DON'T TRY TO PROTECT YOURSELF FROM FEAR

7. LET GO OF ANY FIXED IDENTITY

8. LET GO OF YOUR RELIANCE ON WILLPOWER

9. QUESTION EVERYTHING YOU'VE EVER BEEN TOLD AND EVERYTHING YOU BELIEVE

10. CHOOSE HAPPINESS!

CHAPTER 20
USEFUL REMINDERS

Use this chapter as a reminder of all the key points. If you are unclear on any of them, go to the relevant chapter and read it again.

Chapter 1

You don't have to be a monk to practise mindfulness. Millions of people around the world practise mindfulness today in various forms.

Mindfulness is a tool for achieving a happy state of mind. It is simply a method for seeing things as they really are.

Chapter 2

If you reach the end of the book and you have followed all the instructions in order, you will be ready to enjoy the rest of your life, free from the torment of anxiety and stress, depression, or addiction.

The instructions are not there to control you. They serve only to take the pressure off you. When you follow the instructions, you don't have to convince yourself before moving from step to step. You can relinquish the fight for control.

Chapter 3

Animals lead a more stressful life than humans, yet they don't suffer and die from the effects of stress as we do. They survive by using their senses. When it comes to eating properly and staying fit, we have a lot to learn.

Putting intellect before instinct is the flaw in the incredible human machine. It means we base our perception of reality on thoughts rather than experiences. As a result, we become vulnerable to illusions.

Reality is what is happening to you in the present: the things you can see, hear, smell, taste, and touch. By allowing your mind to become obsessed with thoughts of regret (the past) or anxiety (the future), rather than reality (the present), you invite stress to take the upper hand.

Chapter 4

All the symptoms of addiction are the consequence of intellect overruling instinct.

When you practise mindfulness, you begin to gain clarity as to what is real and what is an illusion.

Chapter 5

When your mind is left to wander, you often become less happy.

Our minds tend to focus on problems and exaggerate them. We create artificial scenarios that cause undue stress.

We typically respond to difficulties in one of three ways:

• Lashing out

• Pretending they don't exist

• Thinking them through

They all cause added stress. Mindfulness is a method whereby you gain control by letting go.

The stressed mind tries to attain happiness by clutching on to pleasant experiences and avoiding painful ones.

While your mind is preoccupied with problems, you ignore the genuine pleasures in life.

Chapter 6

The way we normally respond to physical sensations is very superficial, even to the point of not really feeling at all.

There are three pieces of brainwashing that lead us into the misery of depression, addiction, eating disorders, etc.:

1. The myth that the human mind and body are weak and need outside help in order to enjoy life and cope with stress.

2. The myth that drugs, junk food, etc., can compensate for these illusory weaknesses.

3. The myth that humans are more intelligent than the intelligence that created us, whatever you believe that to be.

Your body is incredibly strong and so are you.

The ability to think means we also have the ability to choose. The reason we so often take the self-destructive option is because we don't always realize we have a choice.

Mindfulness teaches you that there is a lot more to you

than your thoughts. As you learn to pay attention to the evidence of your senses, it brings you into the present and you begin to shake off the assumptions that keep you trapped in the cycle of misery.

Physical sensations are constantly changing. Realizing this can bring a powerful sense of relief. This awareness enables you to make full use of the incredible machine.

Chapter 7

Fixed ideas based on negative thoughts prevent us from seeing things as they really are.

Mindfulness helps us to see the true picture: that everything in life is constantly changing, nothing is permanent and, therefore, everything can be changed for the better.

The normal response to unpleasant feelings is to try to get rid of them, either by grappling with them, trying to think of a solution, or pretending they don't exist. This creates a stressed mindset that makes the unpleasant feelings worse. With mindfulness, you approach difficulties with gentle interest and take in the full picture. This may not make the discomfort go away, but it does avoid adding that extra layer of stress caused by agonizing about it.

By freeing your mind from fixed ideas of yourself and your abilities, you can effect positive physiological changes. In other words, by moving your focus towards good health, strength, dexterity, and hope, you begin to behave accordingly.

The ability to detach yourself from thoughts when you want to and to refocus your mind when it wanders is a skill that can help you greatly reduce stress and anxiety.

Chapter 8

By filling your mind with fixed ideas, perceptions, and assumptions, you fall out of step with experience. Real life moves on and you get left behind.

Drugs, junk food, and all the other so-called 'crutches' that people turn to in the pursuit of happiness do not help; they make matters worse.

When you get stuck with the belief that life is desperate and hard, misery becomes part of your self-image and you behave accordingly.

AS YOU OPEN YOUR MIND AND LET GO OF YOUR ASSUMPTIONS, YOU BECOME AWARE OF THE FULL CAPABILITY OF THE MIND.

When you pay attention to everyday pleasures, you realize that there is plenty to smile about.

By following one simple instruction you can trigger a cycle of awareness and positivity that becomes self-perpetuating. It's the most natural thing in the world.

Clinging to pleasures and hiding from displeasures both create an inaccurate picture of experience. You develop the fear that any pleasure is something you can't live without and any pain is something you can't live with. As a result, both pleasure and pain make you anxious.

With mindfulness, you learn to keep both pleasure and pain in perspective by observing them from a more detached standpoint. This lessens any fear associated with them.

Just by turning your mind towards new ideas you open it up to revelations.

Chapter 9

Fear is the function that triggers a response to danger. It causes us to react in one of three ways: fight, flight, or freeze.

The freeze response can become a permanent state of mind if the perceived danger never goes away. Anxiety takes hold and becomes your everyday condition.

Anyone who feels the need to make a life change will experience the fear of success in some measure. The key is to recognize that it is not a rational fear; it is based on imagination, illusions, and brainwashing.

Chapter 10

Most of the things that we imagine could happen never do because we make sure they don't

Seeing problems coming is one thing; worrying about them is another altogether.

If there is something practical you can do to militate against the likelihood of something bad happening, do it and stop worrying about it. If there's not, then what good is worrying going to do you anyway?

Accept fear as a positive – a function of the incredible machine. That way you will calm your initial response to fear and you will be able to observe more clearly.

Mindfulness does not remove fear from your life altogether. It enables you to accept fear and the vital role it plays, without getting dragged along by it.

See the humour in your own fear.

Positive thinking will reshape the neural pathways in your brain, which in turn will instil a more positive mindset.

Chapter 11

Mindfulness requires no special powers. It unlocks powers you already hold.

With mindfulness, you're not suppressing anything. You're learning to do the opposite, to free your feelings, both positive and negative, so that they are neither suppressed nor exaggerated.

In mindfulness meditation, you learn that not everything that happens in the mind is thinking. The fact that you can be aware of your thoughts shows that thoughts are only part of what is going on in your mind.

As you feel physically stronger and cleaner, your mental happiness will improve. This in turn will have a positive effect on your physical wellbeing and the cycle will turn from a downward spiral of misery to a virtuous circle of happiness.

Detaching from your thoughts does not mean dismissing them and letting go does not mean not bothering. The fact is, without mindfulness, we don't bother a lot of the time. We push feelings and problems aside.

When you accept that you are not the sum of your thoughts you begin to access a new level of mental freedom. You recognize that you are not responsible for everything that happens in your life and you can give yourself a break from having to sort it all out.

Chapter 12

When our thoughts wander to the subject of ourselves, they tend to construct negative identities.

When you allow yourself to get stuck with a fixed perception of yourself, your behaviour starts to conform to that identity.

The mind adapts to experience and new information. Repeated experiences form new patterns of behaviour. But these patterns can be undone again. So the idea that you can or can't do something because of your personality is utterly flawed.

There are two main reasons why we don't stop when we know something is making us unhappy:

1. The fear of success
2. We don't realize we have a choice

Thinking is a wonderful faculty, but it comes with baggage. When you let go of your thoughts, you put down that baggage and observe the thought alone. When you put down the baggage, you remove the layer of panic that accompanies unpleasant thoughts and feelings, thus reducing their impact.

Chapter 13

As soon as you tell yourself you don't have the willpower, you ensure that you will fail.

Using willpower actually makes it harder for you to take control. Your ability to see solutions diminishes when you're stressed.

By letting things be, we allow the natural to take its course and our lives to move with the changes. This leaves us more relaxed and energized, and so much better placed to make sound decisions and see them through.

As long as you continue to believe that you're giving something up, you will always be running in pain. The stronger your will, the longer you will withstand the agony. But the agony only gets worse.

Leaning in to difficulty has been shown to reduce the stress caused by unpleasant experiences.

Chapter 14

When you can see that thoughts are not reality, but just one function of your brain, and that nothing is ever fixed but that everything is always changing, it becomes easier to free yourself from the tug-of-war of fear, address the genuine threats, and free yourself from the fear of imaginary ones.

Be prepared for your moments of anxiety and they won't panic you. By being able to clear your mind from the noise of anxious thoughts, you will be better equipped to:

MAKE GOOD DECISIONS

TAKE POSITIVE ACTIONS

MAKE SOUND JUDGMENTS

HEAR WHAT'S REALLY GOING ON

BE HAPPY

Chapter 15

Practising mindfulness will help you to develop the ability to detach from your thoughts whenever you become aware of them carrying you away into negativity.

Make a point of not letting experiences pass you by without noticing how your body reacts.

Physical and mental wellbeing feed one another.

Whether reality is good or bad, the important thing is to be aware of it.

Reconnect with your physical self, the present, and reality, and you will be better prepared to cope with adversity and enjoy the good times.

Chapter 16

Mindfulness is not about filling your mind with rules and assumptions; it's about freeing your mind and tapping in to your ability to make your own judgments. Mindfulness is first nature. Mindfulness gives you choice.

We define ourselves by what we do rather than who we are, so we try to fill every available second with some sort of doing. The practice of mindfulness teaches us the value of being.

Mindfulness is more natural than the mainstream way of thinking, which effectively allows other people to do your thinking for you.

Explore the full power of your mind. Think for yourself.

Chapter 17

Arm yourself against addiction, even if you have no addictions.

Practise using mindfulness to unravel the myths of addiction. Question the assumptions and determine your own truth.

Close the void between expectation and experience by reconnecting with your senses and thus gaining a more accurate perception of reality.

Chapter 18

Mindfulness does not anaesthetize but heightens sensory perception and leads to a more tuned-in connection with reality.

Reverse the vicious circle of anxiety, tiredness, and stress and turn it into a positive cycle of mindfulness, energy, and happiness.

It's when you relax your grip that the string untangles.

You have a right to happiness. You also have the tools to be happy. Mindfulness unlocks those tools.

It's how you respond to the changing circumstances of life that determines whether you can be happy or not.

Chapter 19

The obsession with *doing* makes us look for constant occupation. This is not relaxing.

Rather than taking out your phone whenever you have a few minutes to kill, practise some of the mindful techniques described in this book. Work them into the most routine activities, such as cooking, eating, and washing, as well as going for walks and taking on creative challenges.

Socialize, express gratitude, and show forgiveness.

Happy relationships are a rich source of personal happiness.

The more you practise mindfulness, the more adept you will become.

It's not realistic to expect to feel happy all the time. What is important is that the thought of unhappiness doesn't cause its own stress. Be prepared for the lows, resist the temptation to cling on to the highs, and accept that life requires a certain amount of rolling with the punches.

ALLEN CARR'S EASYWAY CLINICS

The following list indicates the countries where Allen Carr's Easyway To Stop Smoking Clinics are currently operational.

Check www.allencarr.com for latest additions to this list.

The success rate at the clinics, based on the three-month money-back guarantee, is over 90 per cent.

Selected clinics also offer sessions that deal with alcohol, other drugs and weight issues. Please check with your nearest clinic, listed below, for details.

Allen Carr's Easyway guarantee that you will find it easy to stop at the clinics or your money back.

JOIN US!

Allen Carr's Easyway Clinics have spread throughout the world with incredible speed and success. Our global franchise network now covers more than 150 cities in over 45 countries. This amazing growth has been achieved entirely organically. Former addicts, just like you, were so impressed by the ease with which they stopped that they felt inspired to contact us to see how they could bring the method to their region.

If you feel the same, contact us for details on how to become an Allen Carr's Easyway To Stop Smoking or an Allen Carr's Easyway To Stop Drinking franchisee.

Email us at: **join-us@allencarr.com** including your full name, postal address and region of interest.

SUPPORT US!

No, don't send us money!

You have achieved something really marvellous. Every time we hear of someone escaping from the sinking ship, we get a feeling of enormous satisfaction.

It would give us great pleasure to hear that you have freed yourself from the slavery of addiction so please visit the following web page where you can tell us of your success, inspire others to follow in your footsteps and hear about ways you can help to spread the word.

www.allencarr.com/fanzone

You can "like" our facebook page here
www.facebook.com/AllenCarr

Together, we can help further Allen Carr's mission: to cure the world of addiction.

CLINICS

LONDON CLINIC AND WORLDWIDE HEAD OFFICE

Park House, 14 Pepys Road,
Raynes Park, London SW20 8NH
Tel: +44 (0)20 8944 7761
Fax: +44 (0)20 8944 8619
Email: mail@allencarr.com
Website: www.allencarr.com
Therapists: John Dicey, Colleen Dwyer,
Crispin Hay, Emma Hudson, Rob
Fielding, Sam Kelser, Sam Cleary

Worldwide Press Office

Contact: John Dicey
Tel: +44 (0)7970 88 44 52
Email: media@allencarr.com

UK Clinic Information and Central Booking Line

Tel: 0800 389 2115 (UK only)

UK CLINICS

Birmingham

Tel & Fax: +44 (0)121 423 1227
Therapists: John Dicey, Colleen Dwyer,
Crispin Hay, Rob Fielding
Email: mail@allencarr.com
Website: www.allencarr.com

Brentwood

Tel: 0800 028 7257
Therapists: John Dicey, Colleen Dwyer,
Emma Hudson, Sam Kelser
Email: mail@allencarr.com
Website: www.allencarr.com

Brighton

Tel: 0800 028 7257
Therapists: John Dicey, Colleen Dwyer,
Emma Hudson
Email: mail@allencarr.com
Website: www.allencarr.com

Bristol

Tel: 0800 028 7257
Therapists: John Dicey, Colleen Dwyer,
Emma Hudson, Sam Kelser
Email: mail@allencarr.com
Website: www.allencarr.com

Cambridge

Tel: +44 (0)20 8944 7761
Therapists: Emma Hudson, Sam Kelser
Email: mail@allencarr.com
Website: www.allencarr.com

Coventry

Tel: 0800 321 3007
Therapist: Rob Fielding
Email: info@easywaycoventry.co.uk
Website: www.allencarr.com

Crewe

Tel: +44 (0)1270 664176
Therapist: Debbie Brewer-West
Email: debbie@easyway2stopsmoking.
co.uk
Website: www.allencarr.com

Cumbria

Tel: 0800 077 6187
Therapist: Mark Keen
Email: mark@easywaycumbria.co.uk
Website: www.allencarr.com

Derby

Tel: +44 (0)1270 664176
Therapist: Debbie Brewer-West
Email: debbie@easyway2stopsmoking.
co.uk
Website: www.allencarr.com

Guernsey

Tel: 0800 077 6187
Therapist: Mark Keen
Email: mark@easywaylancashire.co.uk
Website: www.allencarr.com

Isle of Man
Tel: 0800 077 6187
Therapist: Mark Keen
Email: mark@easywaylancashire.co.uk
Website: www.allencarr.com

Jersey
Tel: 0800 077 6187
Therapist: Mark Keen
Email: mark@easywaylancashire.co.uk
Website: www.allencarr.com

Kent
Tel: 0800 028 7257
Therapists: John Dicey, Colleen Dwyer,
Emma Hudson, Sam Kelser
Email: mail@allencarr.com
Website: www.allencarr.com

Lancashire
Tel: 0800 077 6187
Therapist: Mark Keen
Email: mark@easywaylancashire.co.uk
Website: www.allencarr.com

Leeds
Tel: 0800 077 6187
Therapist: Mark Keen
Email: mark@easywayyorkshire.co.uk
Website: www.allencarr.com

Leicester
Tel: 0800 321 3007
Therapist: Rob Fielding
Email: info@easywayleicester.co.uk
Website: www.allencarr.com

Lincoln
Tel: 0800 321 3007
Therapist: Rob Fielding
Email: info@easywayleicester.co.uk
Website: www.allencarr.com

Liverpool
Tel: 0800 077 6187
Therapist: Mark Keen
Email: mark@easywayliverpool.co.uk
Website: www.allencarr.com

Manchester
Tel: 0800 077 6187
Therapist: Mark Keen
Email: mark@easywaymanchester.com
Website: www.allencarr.com

Manchester—alcohol sessions
Tel: +44 (0)7936 712942
Therapist: Mike Connolly
Email: info@stopdrinkingnorth.co.uk
Website: www.allencarr.com

Milton Keynes
Tel: +44 (0)20 8944 7761
Therapists: Emma Hudson, Sam Kelser
Email: mail@allencarr.com
Website: www.allencarr.com

Newcastle/North East
Tel: 0800 077 6187
Therapist: Mark Keen
Email: mark@easywaynortheast.co.uk
Website: www.allencarr.com

Northern Ireland/Belfast
Tel: 0800 077 6187
Therapist: Mark Keen
Email: mark@easywaycumbria.co.uk
Website: www.allencarr.com

Nottingham
Tel: +44 (0)1270 664176
Therapist: Debbie Brewer-West
Email: debbie@easyway2stopsmoking.co.uk
Website: www.allencarr.com

Reading
Tel: 0800 028 7257
Therapists: John Dicey, Colleen Dwyer,
Emma Hudson
Email: info@allencarr.com
Website: www.allencarr.com

SCOTLAND
Glasgow and Edinburgh
Tel: +44 (0)131 449 7858
Therapists: Paul Melvin and Jim
McCreadie

Email: info@easywayscotland.co.uk
Website: www.allencarr.com

Sheffield
Tel: +44 (0)1924 830768
Therapist: Joseph Spencer
Email: joseph@easywaysheffield.co.uk
Website: www.allencarr.com

Shrewsbury
Tel: +44 (0)1270 664176
Therapist: Debbie Brewer-West
Email: debbie@easyway2stopsmoking.co.uk
Website: www.allencarr.com

Southampton
Tel: 0800 028 7257
Therapists: John Dicey, Colleen Dwyer,
Emma Hudson
Email: mail@allencarr.com
Website: www.allencarr.com

Southport
Tel: 0800 077 6187
Therapist: Mark Keen
Email: mark@easywaylancashire.co.uk
Website: www.allencarr.com

Staines/Heathrow
Tel: 0800 028 7257
Therapists: John Dicey, Colleen Dwyer,
Emma Hudson
Email: mail@allencarr.com
Website: www.allencarr.com

Stevenage
Tel: +44 (0)20 8944 7761
Therapists: Emma Hudson, Sam Kelser
Email: mail@allencarr.com
Website: www.allencarr.com

Stoke
Tel: +44 (0)1270 664176
Therapist: Debbie Brewer-West
Email: debbie@easyway2stopsmoking.co.uk
Website: www.allencarr.com

Surrey
Park House, 14 Pepys Road, Raynes Park,
London SW20 8NH
Tel: +44 (0)20 8944 7761
Fax: +44 (0)20 8944 8619
Therapists: John Dicey, Colleen Dwyer,
Crispin Hay, Emma Hudson, Rob Fielding,
Sam Kelser
Email: mail@allencarr.com
Website: www.allencarr.com

Swindon
Tel: 0800 028 7257
Therapists: John Dicey, Colleen Dwyer,
Emma Hudson, Sam Kelser
Email: mail@allencarr.com
Website: www.allencarr.com

Telford
Tel: +44 (0)1270 664176
Therapist: Debbie Brewer-West
Email: debbie@easyway2stopsmoking.co.uk
Website: www.allencarr.com

Watford
Tel: +44 (0)20 8944 7761
Therapists: Emma Hudson, Sam Kelser
Email: mail@allencarr.com
Website: www.allencarr.com

WORLDWIDE CLINICS

REPUBLIC OF IRELAND
Dublin and Cork
Lo-Call (From ROI) 1 890 ESYWAY (37 99 29)
Tel: +353 (0)1 499 9010 (4 lines)
Therapists: Brenda Sweeney and Team
Email: info@allencarr.ie
Website: www.allencarr.com

AUSTRALIA
ACT, NSW, NT, QSL, VIC
Tel: 1300 848 028
Therapist: Natalie Clays
Email: natalie@allencarr.com.au
Website: www.allencarr.com

South Australia
Tel: 1300 848 028
Therapist: Jaime Reed
Email: sa@allencarr.au
Website: www.allencarr.com

Western Australia
Tel: 1300 848 0281
Therapist: Dianne Fisher
Email: wa@allencarr.com.au
Website: www.allencarr.com

AUSTRIA
Sessions held throughout Austria
Freephone: 0800RAUCHEN
(0800 7282436)
Tel: +43 (0)3512 44755
Therapists: Erich Kellermann and Team
Email: info@allen-carr.at
Website: www.allencarr.com

BELGIUM
Antwerp
Tel: +32 (0)3 281 6255
Fax: +32 (0)3 744 0608
Therapist: Dirk Nielandt
Email: info@allencarr.be
Website: www.allencarr.com

BRAZIL
São Paulo
Therapists: Alberto Steinberg &
Lilian Brunstein
Email: contato@easywaysp.com.br
Tel Lilian - (55) (11) 99456-0153
Tel Alberto - (55) (11) 99325-6514
Website: www.allencarr.com

BULGARIA
Tel: 0800 14104 / +359 899 88 99 07
Therapist: Rumyana Kostadinova
Email: rk@nepushaveche.com
Website: www.allencarr.com

CHILE
Tel: +56 2 4744587
Therapist: Claudia Sarmiento

Email: contacto@allencarr.cl
Website: www.allencarr.com

COLOMBIA – Bogota (South America)
Therapist: Felipe Sanint Echeverri
Tel: +57 3158681043
E-mail: info@nomascigarillos.com
Website: www.allencarr.com

CZECH REPUBLIC
Tel: +420 234 261 787
Therapist: Dagmar Janecková
Email: dagmar.janeckova@allencarr.cz
Website: www.allencarr.com

DENMARK
Sessions held throughout Denmark
Tel: +45 70267711
Therapist: Mette Fonss
Email: mette@easyway.dk
Website: www.allencarr.com

ESTONIA
Tel: +372 733 0044
Therapist: Henry Jakobson
Email: info@allencarr.ee
Website: www.allencarr.com

FINLAND
Tel: +358-(0)45 3544099
Therapist: Janne Ström
Email: info@allencarr.fi
Website: www.allencarr.com

FRANCE
Sessions held throughout France
Freephone: 0800 386387
Tel: +33 (4) 91 33 54 55
Email: info@allencarr.fr
Website: www.allencarr.com

GERMANY
Sessions held throughout Germany
Freephone: 08000RAUCHEN
(0800 07282436)
Tel: +49 (0) 8031 90190-0
Therapists: Erich Kellermann and Team

Email: info@allen-carr.de
Website: www.allencarr.com

GREECE
Sessions held throughout Greece
Tel: +30 210 5224087
Therapist: Panos Tzouras
Email: panos@allencarr.gr
Website: www.allencarr.com

GUATEMALA
Tel: +502 2362 0000
Therapist: Michelle Binford
Email: bienvenid@dejedefumarfacil.com
Website: www.allencarr.com

HONG KONG
Email: info@easywayhongkong.com
Website: www.allencarr.com

HUNGARY
Seminars in Budapest and 12 other cities
across Hungary
Tel: 06 80 624 426 (freephone) or
+36 20 580 9244
Therapist: Gabor Szasz
Email: szasz.gabor@allencarr.hu
Website: www.allencarr.com

ICELAND
Reykjavik
Tel: +354 588 7060
Therapist: Petur Einarsson
Email: easyway@easyway.is
Website: www.allencarr.com

INDIA
Bangalore & Chennai
Tel: +91 (0)80 41603838
Therapist: Suresh Shottam
Email: info@easywaytostopsmoking.co.in
Website: www.allencarr.com

IRAN—opening 2017
Tehran and Mashhad
Website: www.allencarr.com

ISRAEL
Sessions held throughout Israel
Tel: +972 (0)3 6212525
Therapists: Ramy Romanovsky,
Orit Rozen
Email: info@allencarr.co.il
Website: www.allencarr.com

ITALY
Sessions held throughout Italy
Tel/Fax: +39 (0)2 7060 2438
Therapists: Francesca Cesati and Team
Email: info@easywayitalia.com
Website: www.allencarr.com

JAPAN
Sessions held throughout Japan
www.allencarr.com

LEBANON
Mob: +961 76 789555
Therapist: Sadek El-Assaad
Email: stopsmoking@allencarreasyway.me
Website: www.allencarr.com

LITHUANIA
Tel: +370 694 29591
Therapist: Evaldas Zvirblis
Email: info@mestirukyti.eu
Website: www.allencarr.com

MAURITIUS
Tel: +230 5727 5103
Therapist: Heidi Hoareau
Email: info@allencarr.mu
Website: www.allencarr.com

MEXICO
Sessions held throughout Mexico
Tel: +52 55 2623 0631
Therapists: Jorge Davo and Mario
Campuzano Otero
Email: info@allencarr-mexico.com
Website: www.allencarr.com

NETHERLANDS
Sessions held throughout the
Netherlands
Allen Carr's Easyway 'stoppen met
roken'
Tel: (+31)53 478 43 62 /
(+31)900 786 77 37
Email: info@allencarr.nl
Website: www.allencarr.com

NEW ZEALAND
North Island – Auckland
Tel: +64 (0)9 817 5396
Therapist: Vickie Macrae
Email: vickie@easywaynz.co.nz
Website: www.allencarr.com

South Island – Dunedin and
Invercargill
Tel: 027 4139 381
Therapist: Debbie Kinder
Email: easywaysouth@icloud.com
Website: www.allencarr.com

NORWAY
Oslo
Tel: +47 93 20 09 11
Therapist: René Adde
Email: post@easyway-norge.no
Website: www.allencarr.com

PERU
Lima
Tel: +511 637 7310
Therapist: Luis Loranca
Email: lloranca@dejardefumaraltoque.com
Website: www.allencarr.com

POLAND
Sessions held throughout Poland
Tel: +48 (0)22 621 36 11
Therapist: Anna Kabat
Email: info@allen-carr.pl
Website: www.allencarr.com

PORTUGAL
Oporto
Tel: +351 22 9958698
Therapist: Ria Slof
Email: info@comodeixardefumar.com
Website: www.allencarr.com

ROMANIA
Tel: +40 (0) 7321 3 8383
Therapist: Diana Vasiliu
Email: raspunsuri@allencarr.ro
Website: www.allencarr.com

RUSSIA
Moscow
Tel: +7 495 644 64 26
Therapist: Alexander Formin
Email: info@allencarr.ru
Website: www.allencarr.com

Crimea, Simferopol
Tel: +38 095 781 8180
Therapist: Yuriy Zhvakolyuk
Email: zhvakolyuk@gmail.com
Website: www.allencarr.com

St Petersburg
Website: www.allencarr.com

SERBIA
Belgrade
Tel: +381 (0)11 308 8686
Email: office@allencarr.co.rs
Website: www.allencarr.com

SINGAPORE
Tel: +65 6329 9660
Therapist: Pam Oei
Email: pam@allencarr.com.sg
Website: www.allencarr.com

SLOVAKIA
Tel: +421 233 04 69 92
Therapist: Peter Sánta
Email: peter.santa@allencarr.sk
Website: www.allencarr.com

SLOVENIA
Tel: 00386 (0) 40 77 61 77
Therapist: Gregor Server
Email: easyway@easyway.si
Website: www.allencarr.com

SOUTH AFRICA
Sessions held throughout South Africa
National Booking Line: 0861 100 200
Head Office: 15 Draper Square,
Draper St, Claremont 7708, Cape Town
Cape Town: Dr Charles Nel
Tel: +27 (0)21 851 5883
Mobile: 083 600 5555
Therapists: Dr Charles Nel, Malcolm
Robinson and Team
Email: easyway@allencarr.co.za
Website: www.allencarr.com

SOUTH KOREA
Seoul
Tel: +82 (0)70 4227 1862
Therapist: Yousung Cha
Email: master@allencarr.co.kr
Website: www.allencarr.com

SWEDEN
Tel: +46 70 695 6850
Therapists: Nina Ljungqvist,
Renée Johansson
Email: info@easyway.se
Website: www.allencarr.com

SWITZERLAND
Sessions held throughout Switzerland
Freephone: 0800RAUCHEN
(0800/728 2436)
Tel: +41 (0)52 383 3773
Fax: +41 (0)52 3833774
Therapists: Cyrill Argast and Team
For sessions in Suisse Romand and
Svizzera Italiana:
Tel: 0800 386 387
Email: info@allen-carr.ch
Website: www.allencarr.com

TURKEY
Sessions held throughout Turkey
Tel: +90 212 358 5307
Therapist: Emre Ustunucar
Email: info@allencarrturkiye.com
Website: www.allencarr.com

UKRAINE
Kiev
Tel: +38 044 353 2934
Therapist: Kirill Stekhin
Email: kirill@allencarr.kiev.ua
Website: www.allencarr.com

UNITED ARAB EMIRATES
Dubai and Abu Dhabi
Tel: +971 56 693 4000
Therapist: Sadek El-Assaad
Email: iwanttoquit@allencarreasyway.me
Website: www.allencarr.com

USA
Denver
Toll free: 1 866 666 4299 /
New York: 212- 330 9194
Email: info@theeasywaytostopsmoking.com
Website: www.allencarr.com
Therapists: Damian O'Hara, Collene
Curran, David Skeist

Houston
Toll free: 1 866 666 4299 / New York:
212- 330 9194
Email: info@theeasywaytostopsmoking.com
Website: www.allencarr.com
Therapists: Damian O'Hara, Collene
Curran, David Skeist

Los Angeles
Toll free: 1 866 666 4299 / New York:
212- 330 9194
Email: info@theeasywaytostopsmoking.com
Website: www.allencarr.com
Therapists: Damian O'Hara, Collene
Curran, David Skeist

Milwaukee (and South Wisconsin)—opening 2017
Website: www.allencarr.com

New Jersey—opening 2017
Website: www.allencarr.com

New York
Toll free: 1 866 666 4299 /
New York: 212- 330 9194
Email: info@theeasywaytostopsmoking.com
Website: www.allencarr.com
Therapists: Damian O'Hara, Collene
Curran, David Skeist

CANADA
Sessions held throughout Canada
Toll free: +1-866 666 4299 /
+1 905 849 7736
English Therapist: Damian O'Hara
French Therapist: Rejean Belanger
Email: info@theeasywaytostopsmoking.
com
Website: www.allencarr.com

OTHER ALLEN CARR PUBLICATIONS

Allen Carr's revolutionary Easyway method is available in a wide variety of formats, including digitally as audiobooks and ebooks, and has been successfully applied to a broad range of subjects.

For more information about Easyway publications, please visit
shop.allencarr.com

Stop Smoking with Allen Carr
(with 70-minute audio CD)

Stop Smoking Now
(with hypnotherapy CD)

**Your Personal
Stop Smoking Plan**

The Easy Way to Stop Smoking

**The Easy Way for Women to
Stop Smoking**

**Easyway Express: Stop
Smoking and Quit E-cigarettes**
(ebook)

**The Only Way to Stop Smoking
Permanently**

**The Illustrated Easy Way to
Stop Smoking**

**The Illustrated Easy Way for
Women to Stop Smoking**

The Nicotine Conspiracy
(ebook)

How to Be a Happy Nonsmoker
(ebook)

No More Ashtrays

Finally Free!

**How to Stop Your Child
Smoking**

The Little Book of Quitting

**Smoking Sucks (Parent Guide
with 16 page pull-out comic)**
(ebook)

Stop Drinking Now
(with hypnotherapy CD)

**The Easy Way to Control
Alcohol**

**Your Personal Stop Drinking
Plan**

**The Illustrated Easy Way to
Stop Drinking**

**The Easy Way for Women to
Stop Drinking**

No More Hangovers

Lose Weight Now
(with hypnotherapy CD)

No More Diets

The Easy Way for Women to Lose Weight

Good Sugar Bad Sugar

The Easy Way to Stop Gambling

No More Gambling
(ebook)

Get Out of Debt Now

No More Debt
(ebook)

The Easy Way to Enjoy Flying

No More Fear of Flying

Burning Ambition

No More Worrying

Packing It In The Easy Way
(the autobiography)

Want Easyway on your **smartphone** or **tablet**?
Search for "Allen Carr" in your app store.

Easyway publications are also available as audiobooks.
Visit **shop.allencarr.com** to find out more.